Atlas of the
World

D1485914

GEDDES & GROSSET

2 **CONTENTS**

4-5	THE WORLD
6-27	NORTH & CENTRAL AMERICA
28-41	SOUTH AMERICA
42-95	EUROPE
96-133	ASIA
134-151	AFRICA
152-165	AUSTRALIA & OCEANIA
166-171	THE POLAR REGIONS
172	INDEX TO MAPS

ads

Motorway/Highway

Other Main Road

scales smaller than 1 : 3 million

Principal Road: Motorway/Highway

Other Main Road

Main Railway

ns & Cities - Population

> 5,000,000

1-5,000,000

500,000-1,000,000

< 500,000

aris National Capital

✈ Airport

International Boundary

International Boundary
- not defined or in dispute

Internal Boundary

River

Canal

Marsh or Swamp

Relief

Note -

The 0-100 contour layer
appears only at scales
larger than 1 : 3 million

1510 Peak (in meters)

5000 meters
4000
3000
2000
1000
500
200
100
0
Land below sea level

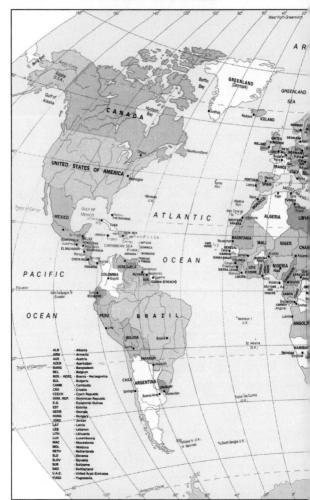

ALB	- Albania
ARM	- Armenia
AUS	- Austria
AZER	- Azerbaijan
BANG	- Bangladesh
BEL	- Belgium
BOS. - HERZ.	- Bosnia - Hersegovina
BUL.	- Bulgaria
CAMB	- Cambodia
CRO	- Croatia
CZECH	- Czech Republic
DOM. REP.	- Dominican Republic
E.G.	- Equatorial Guinea
EST	- Estonia
GEOR	- Georgia
HUNG	- Hungary
JORD.	- Jordan
LAT	- Latvia
LEB	- Lebanon
LITH	- Lithuania
LUX	- Luxembourg
MAC	- Macedonia
MOL.	- Moldova
NETH	- Netherlands
SLO	- Slovenia
SLOV	- Slovakia
SUR	- Surinam
SWZ	- Switzerland
U.A.E.	- United Arab Emirates
YUGO	- Yugoslavia

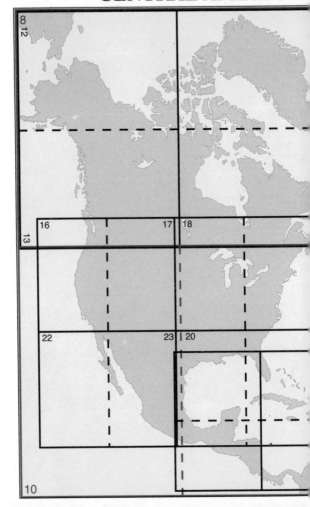

8-9 NORTH AMERICA
POLITICAL (N)

10-11 NORTH AMERICA
POLITICAL (S)

12-13 CANADA (W)

14-15 CANADA (E)

16-17 U.S.A. (N.W.)

18-19 U.S.A. (N.E.)

20-21 U.S.A. (S.E.) & WESTERN
CARIBBEAN

22-23 U.S.A. (S.W.), MEXICO, ALASKA
& HAWAIIAN ISLANDS

24-25 CENTRAL AMERICA

26-27 EASTERN CARIBBEAN

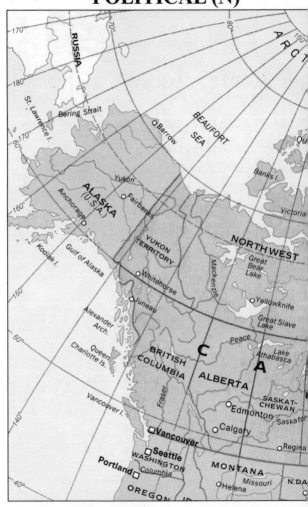

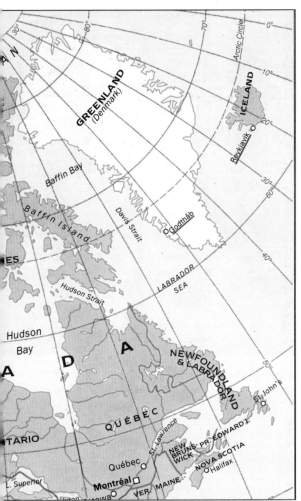

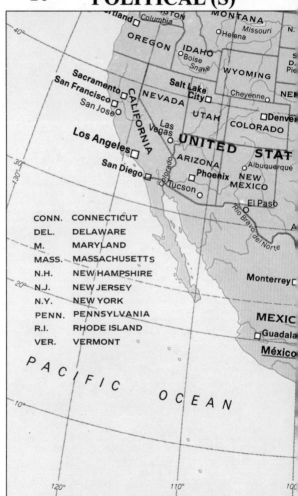

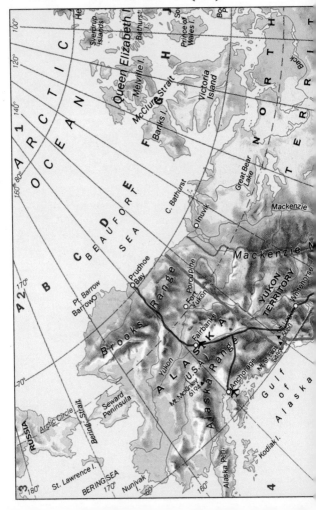

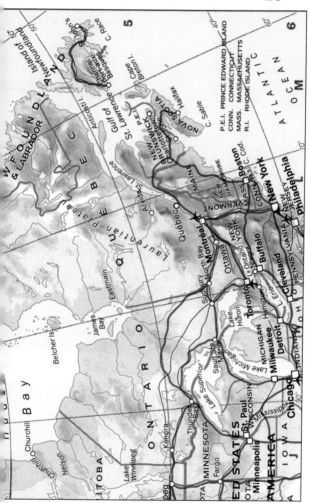

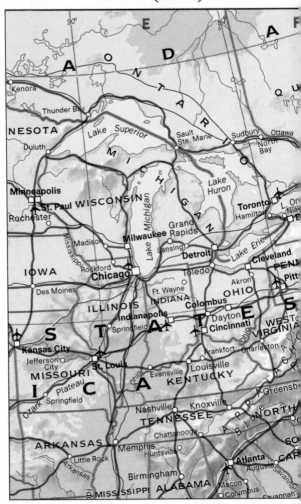

CONN.	CONNECTICUT
MASS.	MASSACHUSETTS
R.I.	RHODE ISLAND
N.J.	NEW JERSEY
DEL.	DELAWARE

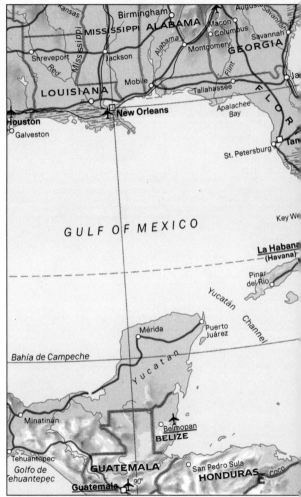

OCEAN

3

Guadalupe (Mex.)

A

120°

Mana Kauai

Niihau

Kauai Channel

Oahu **H**

Wahiawa Kaneohe

Honolulu

Molokai Kalaupapa

B

Lanai Wailuka

PACIFIC 305? Maui

OCEAN

Kahoolawe

Alenuihaha Channel

Kawaihae -20°

HAWAIIAN ISLANDS

1 : 10 000 000

0 ——— 200 km
0 ——— 100 miles

Kailua 4205▲ Hilo

4169▲

Hawaii

Pahala

155°

160°

Tro

ALASKA

1 : 40 000 000

0 ——— 800 km
0 ——— 400 miles

RUSSIA

70° 170° 160° 150° Prudhoe Ba

Arctic Circle Brooks Range

ALASKA

(U.S.A.

80° Bering Strait Fairbanks

St. Lawrence I. Yukon Range

J 6194▲ Mt McKinley Anchora

Alaska Range

BERING SEA

Near Gulf o

Islands Alask

Kodiak I.

Aleutian Islands

50° 180° Unimak I. 160° 150°

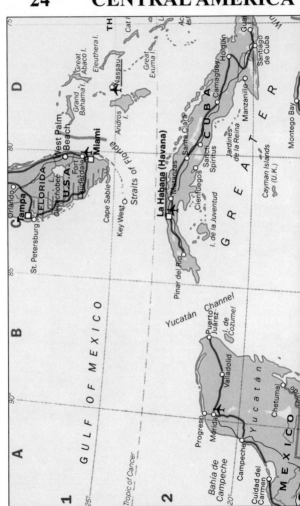

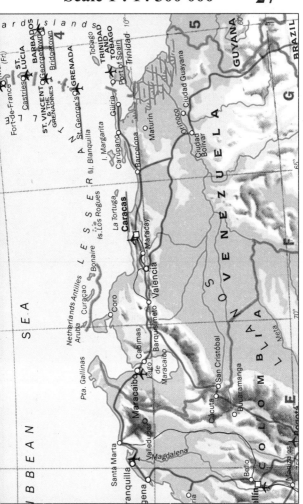

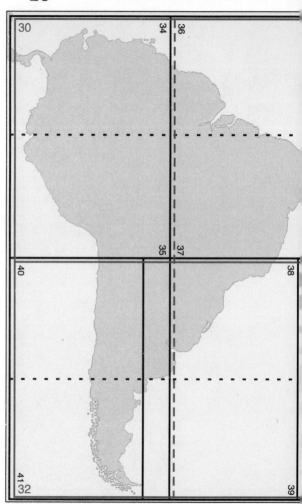

30 · 34 · 36 · 35 · 37 · 40 · 41 · 32 · 38 · 39

Martinique (Fr.)

ST. VINCENT
& THE GRENADINES

GRENADA

NICARAGUA

Netherlands
Antilles

Curaçao

Güiria

80°

70°

10°

COSTA
RICA

Barranquilla

Maracaibo

Caracas

Barcelona

Panamá

Cartagena

Barquisimeto

PANAMA

Monteria

L. Maracaibo

Rinoco

VENEZUELA

Medellín

Bogotá

COLOMBIA

Boa Vis

Cali

Negro

0° Equator

Quito

Japurá

Manta

ECUADOR

Guayaquil

Amazonas

Loja

Iquitos

B   R   A

Ucayali

Cruzeiro do
Sul

Lábrea

Hum

Trujillo

Rio Branco

Pôrto V

PERU

Madre de Dios

Mamoré

10°

Callao

Huancayo

Lima

Cuzco

L. Titicaca

Arequipa

La Paz

BOLIVIA

Oruro

San
Cru

Arica

Sucre

20°

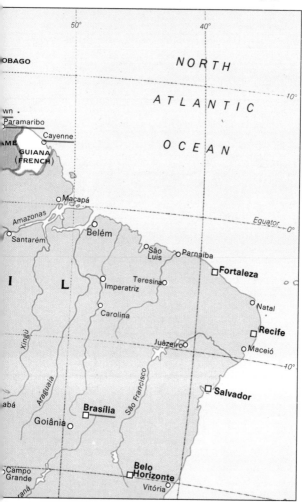

OBAGO

NORTH

ATLANTIC

10°

wn
Paramaribo

Cayenne

AME
GUIANA
(FRENCH)

OCEAN

Macapá

Equator   0°

Amazonas

Belém

Santarém

São
Luis

Parnaiba

Fortaleza

I

L

Teresina

Imperatriz

Natal

Carolina

Recife

Juàzeiro

Maceió

10°

Xingú

Araguaia

São Francisco

Salvador

abá

Brasília

Goiânia

Campo
Grande

Belo
Horizonte

Vitória

50°   40°

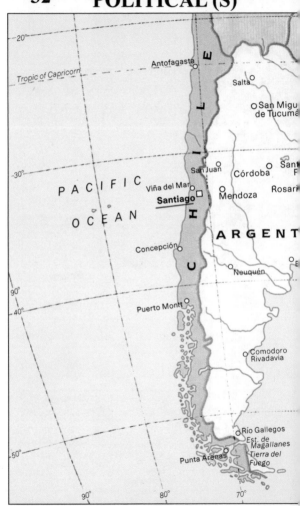

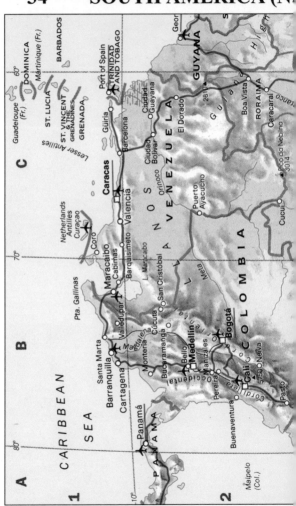

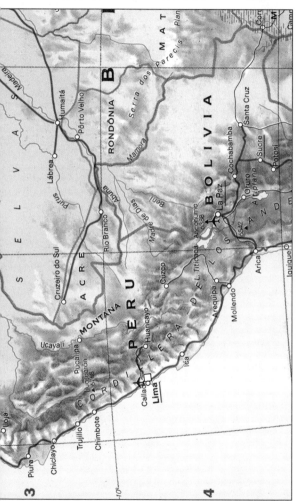

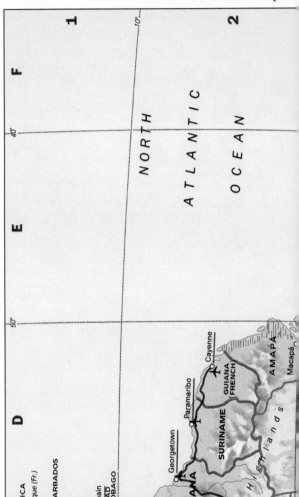

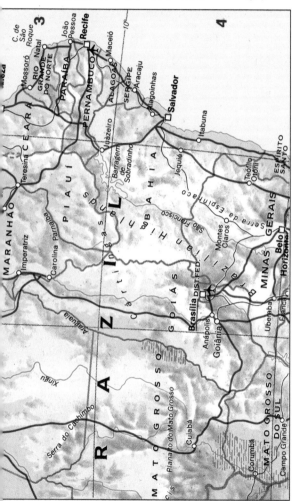

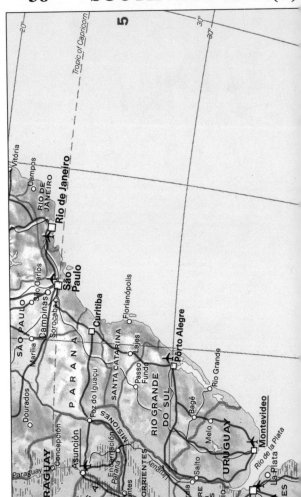

ATLANTIC

OCEAN

South Georgia
(U.K.)

nds
as) Stanley
East
Falkland

7

8

G

F

E

D

40°

50°

20°

30°

40°

50°

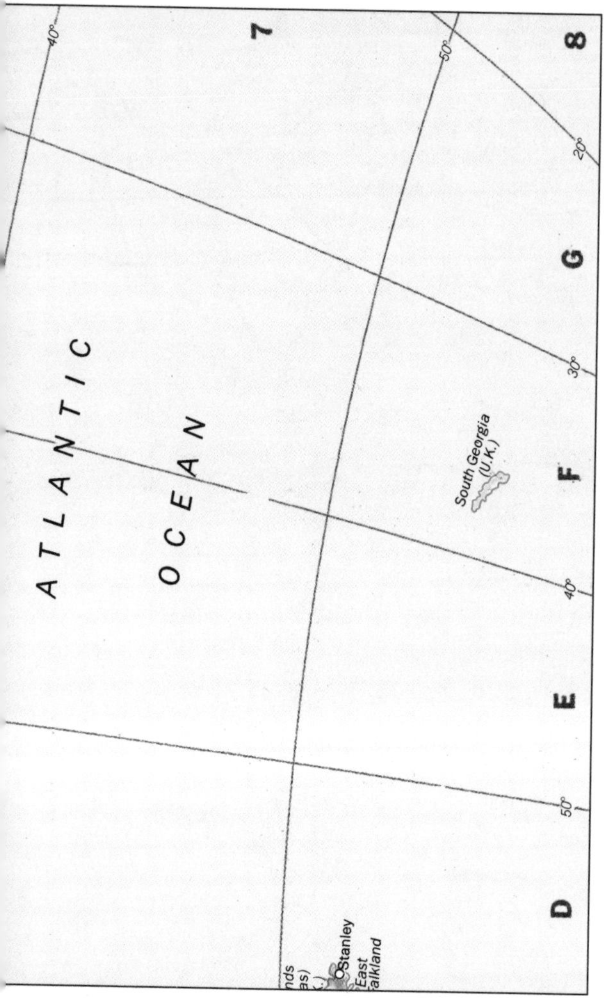

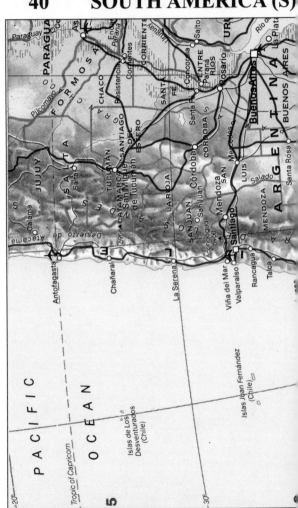

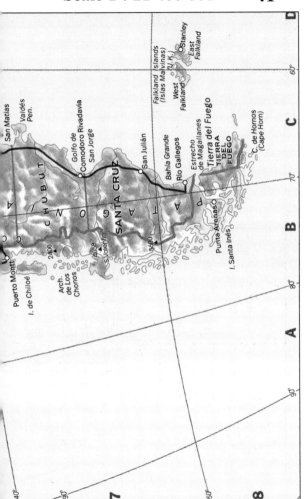

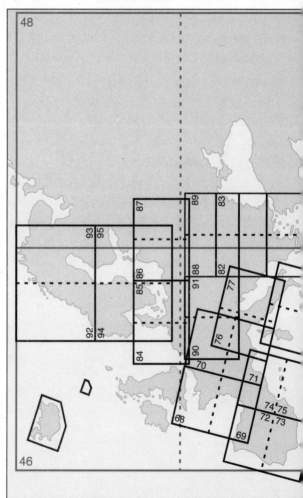

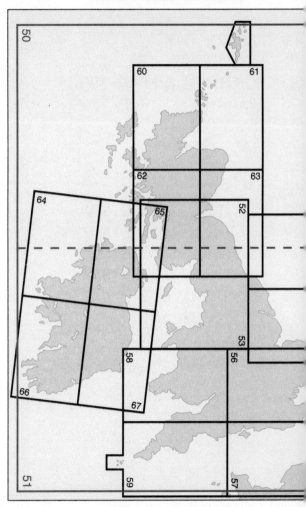

47 EUROPE POLITICAL (W)
49 EUROPE POLITICAL (S)
51 BRITISH ISLES
53 ENGLAND & WALES (N.W.)
55 ENGLAND (N.E.)
57 ENGLAND (N.S.)
59 ENGLAND & WALES (N.S.)
61 SCOTLAND (N)
63 SCOTLAND (S)
65 IRELAND (N)
67 IRELAND (S)

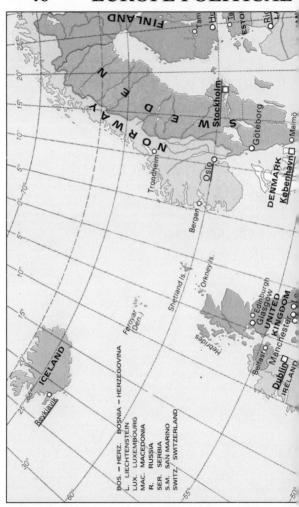

FINLAND

N O R W A Y

S W E D E N

Stockholm

Göteborg

Malmö

Oslo

Trondheim

DENMARK
København

Bergen

Orkney Is.

Shetland Is.

Edinburgh
Glasgow
UNITED
KINGDOM
Manchester

Hebrides

Belfast
Dublin
IRELAND

Føroyar
(Dan.)

ICELAND

Reykjavík

BOS. – HERZ. BOSNIA – HERZEGOVINA
L.   LIECHTENSTEIN
LUX. LUXEMBOURG
MAC. MACEDONIA
R.   RUSSIA
SER. SERBIA
S.M. SAN MARINO
SWITZ. SWITZERLAND

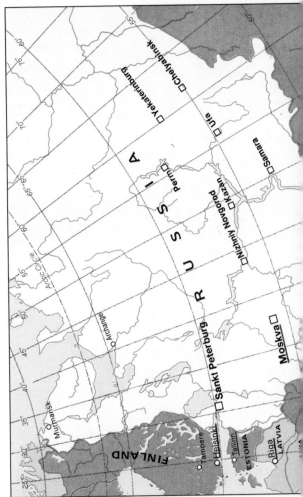

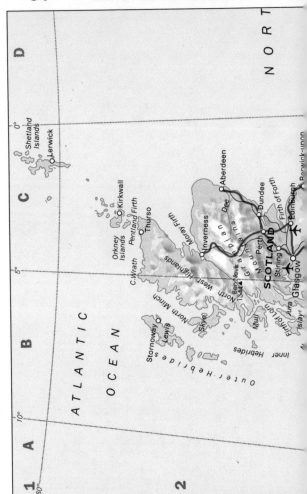

NORTH

0°

Shetland Islands
Lerwick

Kirkwall
Orkney Islands
Pentland Firth
Thurso
C.Wrath

Aberdeen
Dundee
Dee
Firth of Forth
Edinburgh
Berwick-upon

Inverness
Moray Firth
Grampian
West Highlands
North West Highlands
Ben Nevis 1344
SCOTLAND
Perth
Stirling
Glasgow

ATLANTIC
OCEAN

Stornoway
Lewis
North Minch
Skye
Mull
Jura
Islay
Firth of Lorn
Inner Hebrides
Outer Hebrides

D
C
B
A

1
2

60°
70°
5°

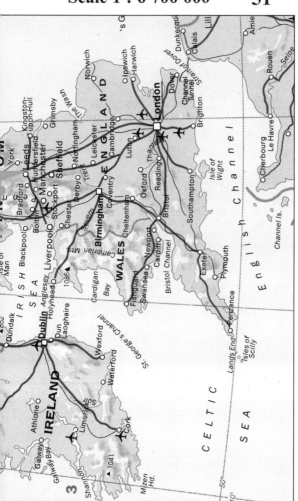

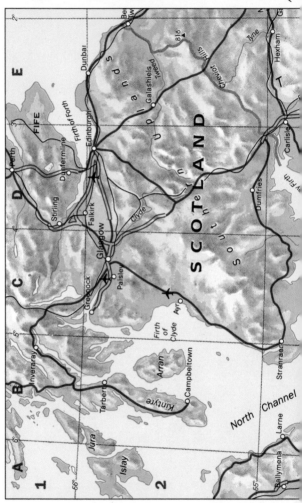

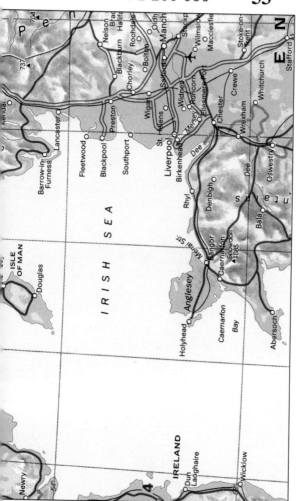

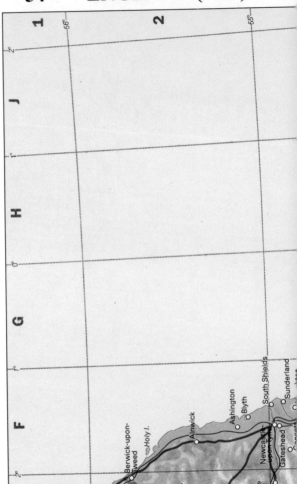

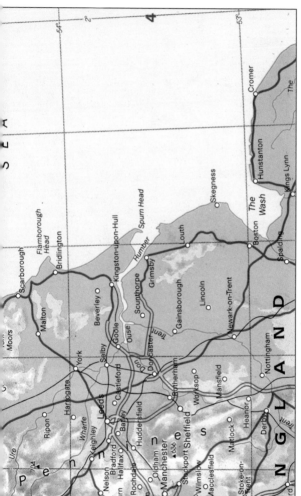

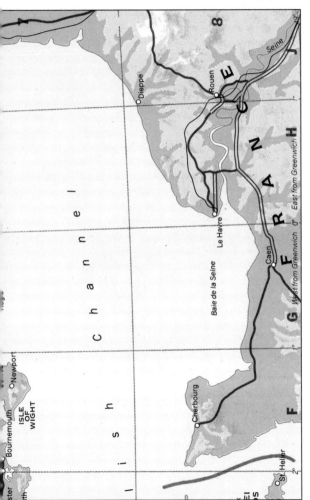

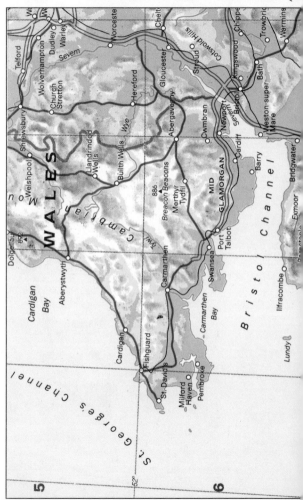

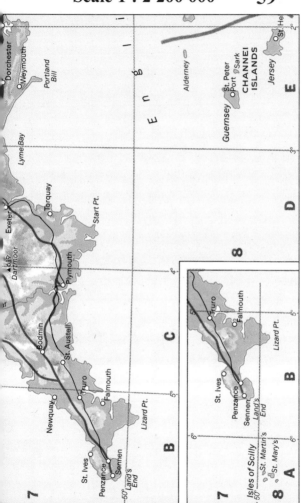

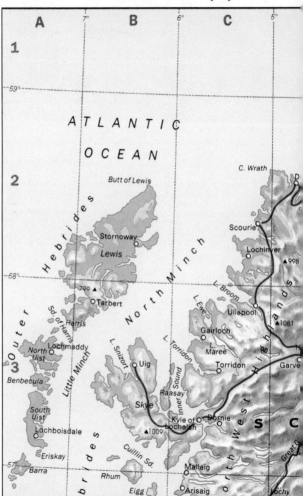

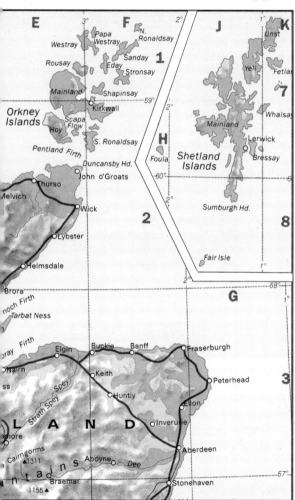

E

Westray
Papa Westray
N. Ronaldsay
Rousay
Eday
Sanday
Stronsay
Mainland
Shapinsay
1
Kirkwall
Orkney Islands
Scapa Flow
Hoy
S. Ronaldsay
Pentland *Firth*
Duncansby Hd.
John o'Groats
Melvich
Thurso
Wick
2
Lybster
Helmsdale
Brora
noch *Firth*
Tarbat Ness

J
Unst
K
Yell
Fetlar
7
Whalsa
Mainland
Lerwick
H
Shetland Islands
Bressay
Foula
Sumburgh Hd.
8
Fair Isle

G

ray *Firth*
Elgin
Buckie
Banff
Fraserburgh
Nairn
Keith
ss
Strath Spey
Huntly
Peterhead
Spey
Ellon
Inverurie
3
L A N D
Aberdeen
hore
Cairngorms ▲1311
ntains
Aboyne
Dee
1155 ▲
Braemar
Stonehaven

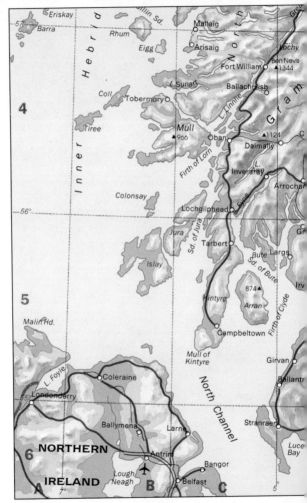

Eriskay
Barra
Rhum
Sgurr Sd.
Eigg
Mallaig
Arisaig
Lochy
Ben Nevis ▲1344
Fort William
Hebrides
Inner
L. Sunart
Ballachulish
Coll
Tobermory
North
Gram
Tiree
Mull ▲966
Oban
Dalmally ▲1124
L. Linnhe
Firth of Lorn
L. Inveraray
Colonsay
Arrochar
Lochgilphead
Jura
Tarbert
Sd. of Jura
Largs
Bute
Sd. of Bute
Gr
Islay
874▲
Arran
Irv
Malin Hd.
Kintyre
Campbeltown
Firth of Clyde
Mull of
Kintyre
Girvan
Coleraine
North Channel
Ballantr
Londonderry
L. Foyle
Ballymena
Larne
Stranraer
Luce
Bay
NORTHERN
Antrim
IRELAND
Lough
Neagh
Bangor
Belfast
A 7° B 6° C 5°

e Cairngo
▲1311
ntains Aboyne Dee
1155▲ Braemar
Stonehaven 57°
Laurencekirk
Blair Atholl
Pitlochry Montrose
Dunkeld Forfar
Tay Arbroath
ieff Perth Dundee 4
Earn Firth of Tay
Cupar St. Andrews
Ochil Hills Fife Ness
Stirling Glenrothes
Dunfermline Kirkcaldy N O R T H
Falkirk Firth of Forth
Edinburgh Dunbar S E A
atbridge Livingston Musselburgh 56°
St. Abb's Hd.
therwell
Lanark Berwick-upon
Peebles Uplands -Tweed
Clyde Galashiels Tweed
Jedburgh ▲816 5
thern Hawick Alnwick
Moffat Teviothead Cheviot Hills
Tyne
Dumfries
Gretna Newcastle- 55°
-upon-Tyne South
Carlisle E N G L A N D Shields
Solway Firth Durham
Eden 6
Penrith
E 3° F 2° Tees G

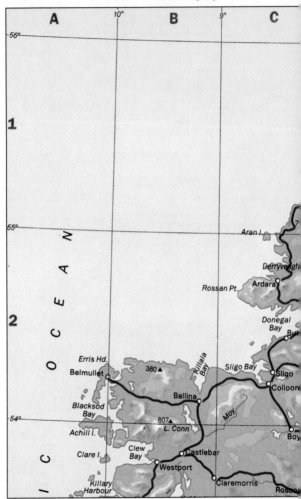

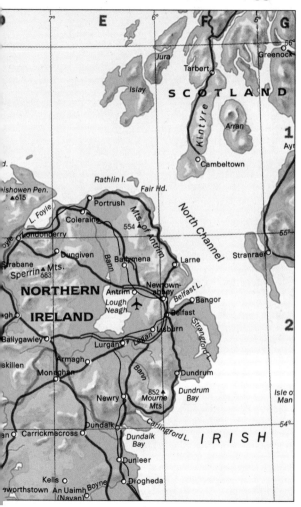

E   6°   F   6°   G

Jura

Tarbert

Greenock

SCOTLAND

Islay

Kintyre

Arran

1

Ayr

Cambeltown

Rathlin I.

Fair Hd.

~Ishowen Pen.
▲615

Portrush

Mts of Antrim

North Channel

L. Foyle

Coleraine

554▲

55°

Londonderry

Stranraer

Dungiven

Bann

Ballymena

Larne

Foyle

Srabane
Sperrin ▲ Mts.
583

Newtown-
abbey

Belfast L.

NORTHERN

Antrim

Bangor

Lough
Neagh

Belfast

gh

IRELAND

Lisburn

Strangford L.

Ballygawley

Lurgan

Lagan

2

Armagh

skillen

Monaghan

Bann

Dundrum

Newry

852▲
Mourne
Mts

Dundrum
Bay

Isle o
Man

Dundalk

Carlingford L.

54°

an   Carrickmacross

Dundalk
Bay

IRISH

Dunleer

Kells

Drogheda

eworthstown   An Uaimh
(Navan)

Boyne

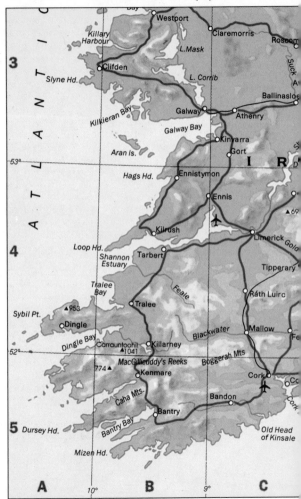

3

Bay

Westport

Claremorris

Roscom

Killary
Harbour

L. Mask

Slyne Hd.

Clifden

L. Corrib

Ballinasloe

Kilkieran Bay

Galway

Athenry

Galway Bay

Kinvarra

Gort

Aran Is.

I   **R**

53°

Hags Hd.

Ennistymon

Ennis

▲69

Kilrush

Limerick

Gola

4

Loop Hd.

Shannon
Estuary

Tarbert

Tipperary

Tralee
Bay

Feale

Ráth Luirc

Sybil Pt.

▲953

Dingle

Tralee

Blackwater

Mallow

Fe

Dingle Bay

Carrauntoohil
▲1041

Killarney

Boggerah Mts.

52°

MacGillicuddy's Reeks

774 ▲

Kenmare

Cork

Cc

Caha Mts.

Bandon

Cork

5

Dursey Hd.

Bantry

Bantry Bay

Old Head
of Kinsale

Mizen Hd.

A   10°   **B**   9°   **C**

A T L A N T I C

Kells
worthstown   An Uaimh   Boyne   Drogheda
(Navan)
Balbriggan
Mullingar
Kinnegad
SEA
3
Tullamore
Bog of Allen   Liffey   Dublin
Howth Hd.
Dublin
Bay
Dun Laoghaire
Naas   Bray
Kildare
850 ▲
L   A   N   D
Wicklow
53°
926 ▲   Wicklow Hd.
Wicklow Mts
Carlow
Kilkenry
Slaney
Arklow
4
Enniscorthy
Wexford
Bay
New Ross
Wexford
Rosslare
Waterford
Carnsore Pt.
arvan
Waterford Harbour
S t . G e o r g e ' s   C h a n n e l
52°
Fishguard
WALES
5
Barrow

7°   **E**   6°   **F**   5°

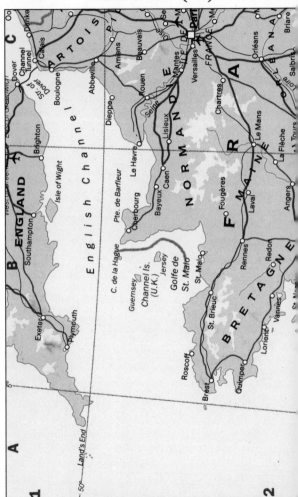

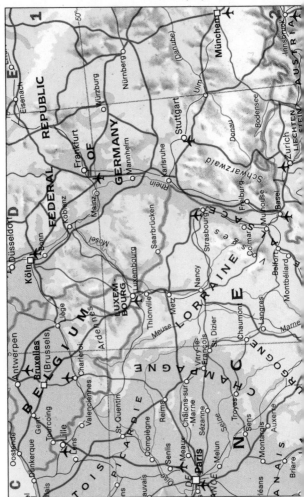

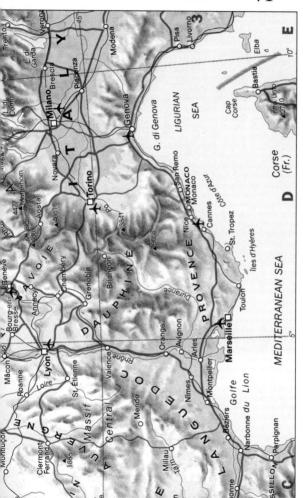

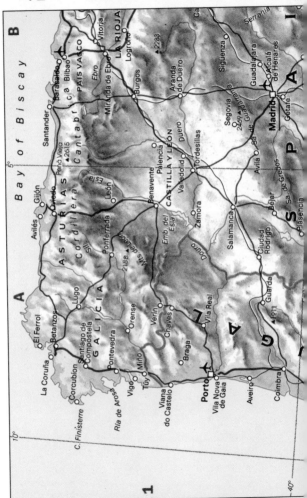

Bay of Biscay

B

Serrania

▲2283

Vitoria
LA RIOJA
Logroño

Siguenza

Guadalajara

Alcalá
de Henares

PAIS VASCO

Baracaldo

C.ª Bilbao

Ebro

Miranda de Ebro

Burgos

Aranda
de Duero

Duero

Madrid

Getafe

S   P   A

Santander

Peña Vieja
▲2615

C a n t a b r

Segovia
▲2469
S.ª de Guadarrama

Avila

S.ª de Gredos

Béjar

Palencia

CASTILLA Y LEÓN

Valladolid

Tordesillas

Plasencia

Gijón

Aviles

Oviedo

ASTURIAS

Cordillera

Esla

León

Benavente

Zamora

Salamanca

Ciudad
Rodrigo

Guarda

▲1991

El Ferrol

La Coruña

Betanzos

Lugo

Sil

Ponferrada

Mtes. de León
▲2188

Emb. del
Esla

Douro

A

C. Finisterre

Corcubión

Santiago de
Compostela

GALICIA

Pontevedra

Orense

Verín

Chaves

Vila Real

U

Ría de Arosa

Vigo

Miño

Túy

Braga

I

Viana
do Castelo

Porto

Vila Nova
de Gaia

Aveiro

Coimbra

10°

40°

1

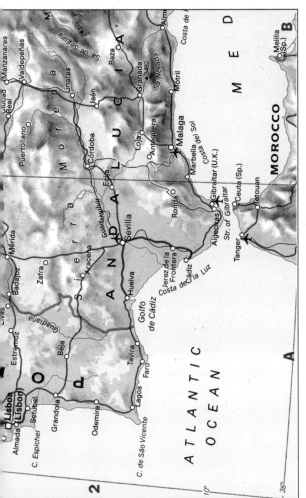

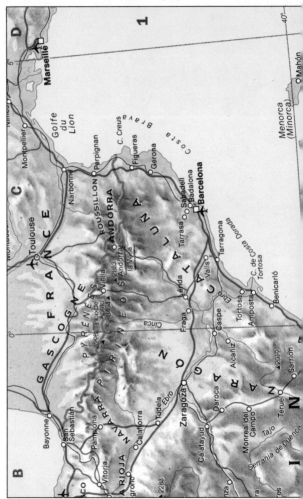

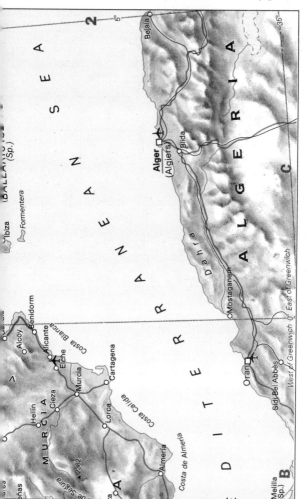

A L G E R I A

Bejaia

Alger □ ⌖
(Algiers)

Blida

C

Dahra

Mostaganem

Oran □ ⌖

Sidi-Bel-Abbès

West of Greenwich │ East of Greenwich

M E D I T E R R A N E A N   S E A

(BALEARIC)
Ibiza (Sp.)

Formentera

2

6°

36°

Benidorm

Alcoy

Alicante

Costa Blanca

Elche

Murcia

Cartagena

Cieza

M U R C I A

Hellín

Lorca

Costa Cálida

▲2382

de Segura

Almería

Costa de Almería

Melilla
(Sp.)

B

A

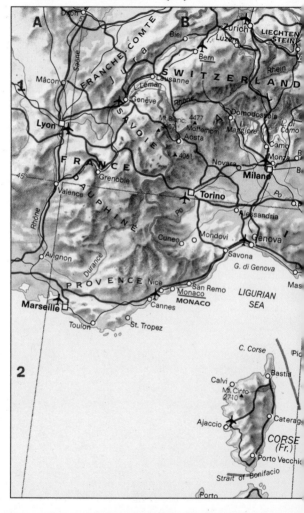

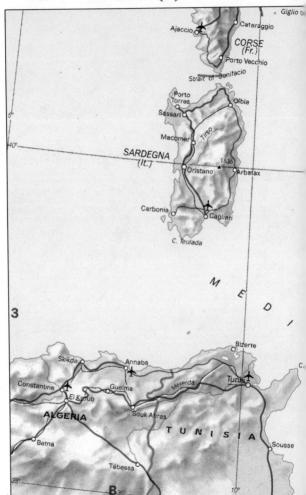

Giglio

Ajaccio ✈ Cateraggio

CORSE
(Fr.)

Porto Vecchio

Strait of Bonifacio

Porto
Torres
Olbia

Sassari

Macomer
Tirso

SARDEGNA
(It.)
1836

Oristano Arbatax

Carbonia
Cagliari

C. Teulada

M E D I

3

Bizerte

Skikda Annaba

Constantine Tunis
El Kroub Guelma Mejerda

ALGERIA Souk Ahras

T U N I S I A

Batna Sousse

Tébessa

B 35°

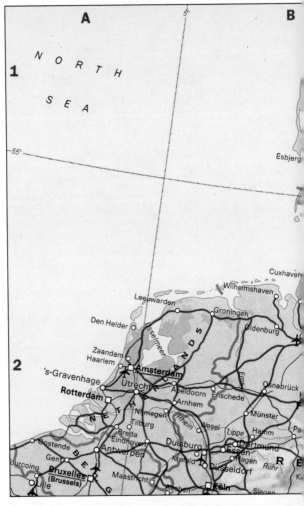

A

B

5°

N O R T H

S E A

1

55°

Esbjerg

Cuxhaven

Wilhelmshaven

Leeuwarden

Groningen

Den Helder

Oldenburg

Zaandam

Haarlem

Amsterdam

's-Gravenhage

Utrecht

Apeldoorn

Enschede

Osnabrück

2

Rotterdam

Arnhem

Ems

Nijmegen

Rhein

Wesel

Münster

Tilburg

Lippe

Hamm

Breda

Eindhoven

Duisburg

Oostende

Gent

Antwerpen

Krefeld

Essen

Dortmund

Hagen

R

Bruxelles
(Brussels)

Maastricht

Düsseldorf

Ruhr

K

ourcoing

Lille

Aachen

Köln

Siegen

Leeuwarden

IJsselmeer

N E T H E R L A N D S

B E L G

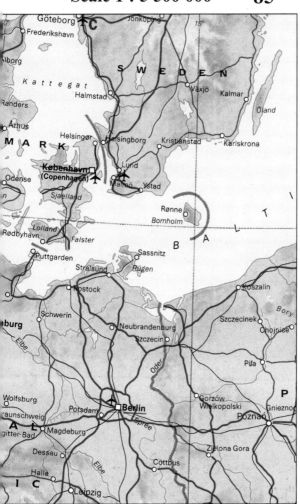

D

Visby
Gotland

Gulf of Riga

E

20°

25°

Ventspils

Riga

Jelgava

Dvina

S
E
A

Liepāja

Šiauliai

Pane

Klaipeda

LITHUANIA

Šilute

Kaunas

Gulf of
Danzig

Kaliningrad

Gusev

Gdynia

RUSSIA

Gdańsk

Elblag

Augustow

Grodno

Olsztyn

Tucholskie

Wisła

Grudziadz

Bydgoszcz

Toruń

Mława

Białystok

O L A N D

Bug

Włocławek

Warszawa
(Warsaw)

Siedlce

Brest

Konin

Kalisz

Łódź

Radom

Lublin

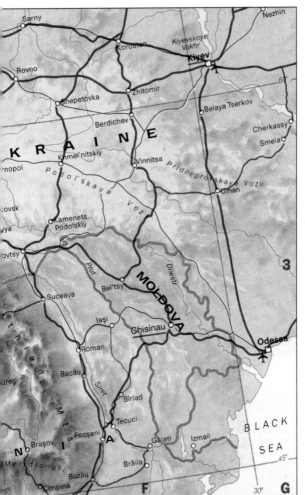

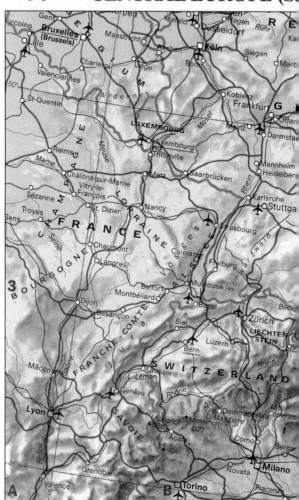

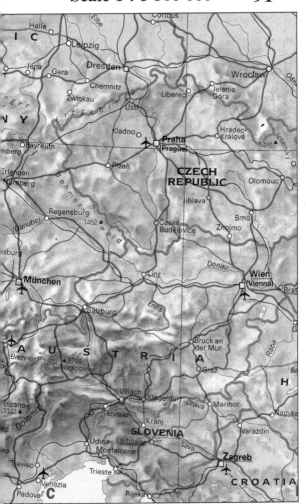

A 25° 20° Grimsey **B** 15° Arctic Circle **C**

Ísafjördhur

▲845

Húna-flói

○Húsavik

Blöndúós ○Akureyri

1 Seydhisfjördhur

65° I C E L A N D 65°

Faxaflói ▲1765 ▲1833

25° Vatnajökull

Reykjavik ○Kópavogur Höfn ○

2 Keflavík 2119▲ 15°

○Hella

Vestmannaeyjar

ICELAND
Same scale

●Surtsey 20°

Same scale 7° 10° Arctic Circle

Streymoy

62° ○Tórshavn Bodö ○

Faeroe Is. Sandoy

Suduroy ○Mo i Ra

FØROYAR
(FAEROES)
(Denmark) 7° Mosjöen ▲17

65°

5°

N O R W E G I A N Grong ○

1390▲

Steinkjer

S E A Strömsund

Trondheim Storlien Östers

Molde ○ Storsjön ○

3 Ålesund ○ Stören ○ Br

2286▲ ○Oppdal 1710▲

Glitterind ○Dombås Femunden

2470 Sveg ○ **E**

○Otta

Lofoten Vesterål

Vestfjorden

Trøndelag

Trondheim fish

Nordfj

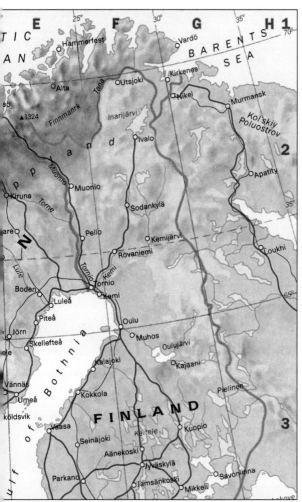

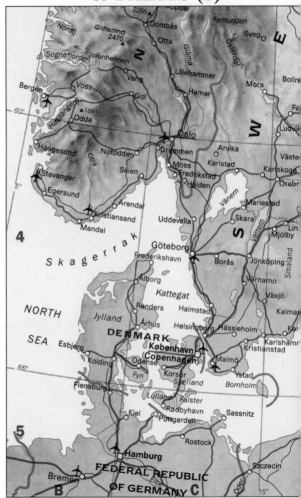

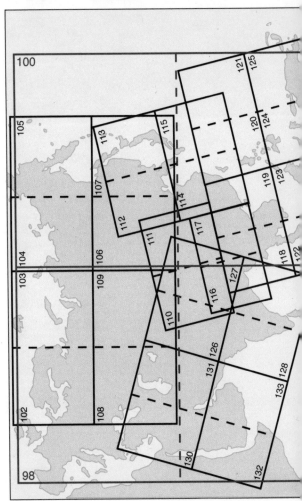

-99	ASIA POLITICAL (W)
0-101	ASIA POLITICAL (E)
2-103	RUSSIA (N.W.)
4-105	RUSSIA (N.E.)
6-107	RUSSIA (S.E.)
8-109	RUSSIA (S.W.)
0-111	EASTERN ASIA (N.W.)
2-113	EASTERN ASIA (N.E.)
4-115	EASTERN ASIA (S.E.), CENTRAL JAPAN
5-117	EASTERN ASIA (S.W.)
8-119	S.E. ASIA (W)
0-121	S.E. ASIA (E)
2-123	MALAYSIA & INDONESIA (W)
4-125	INDONESIA (E)
5-127	NORTHERN INDIA & THE HIMALAYAS
8-129	SOUTHERN INDIA
0-131	MIDDLE EAST (N)
2-133	MIDDLE EAST (S)

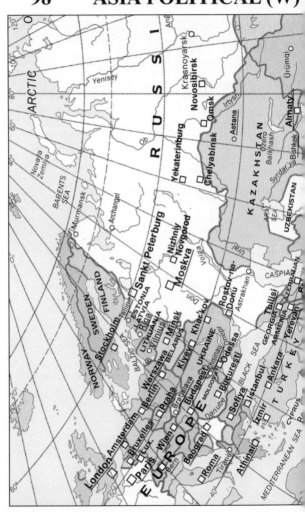

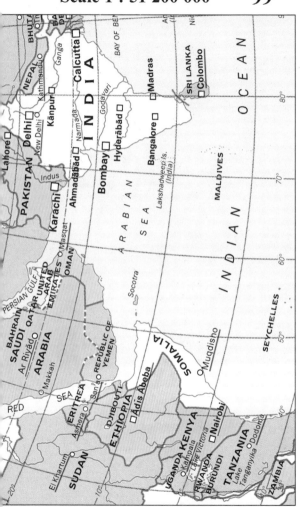

JAPAN

TŌKYŌ
Yokohama
Osaka
Sapporo
Hokkaido
Honshū

SEA OF JAPAN

NORTH KOREA
SOUTH KOREA
Sōul
Kitakyūshū
Kyūshū

Harbin
Changchun
Shenyang
Pyōngyang
Beijing
Tianjin

MONGOLIA
Ulaanbaatar

Kuril Is.
Sakhalin
Vladivostok
Khabarovsk
Magadan

SEA OF OKHOTSK

BERING SEA

Aleutian Is.

OCEAN

Amur
Lena
Yakutsk
Ozero Baykal
Irkutsk
Angara
...arsk

Tropic of Cancer

ARCTIC CIRCLE

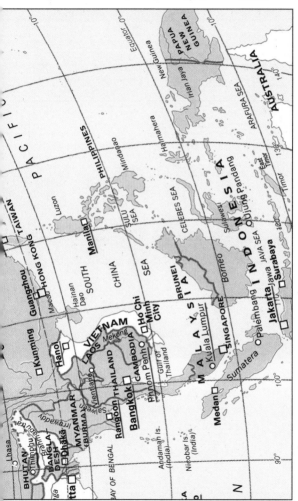

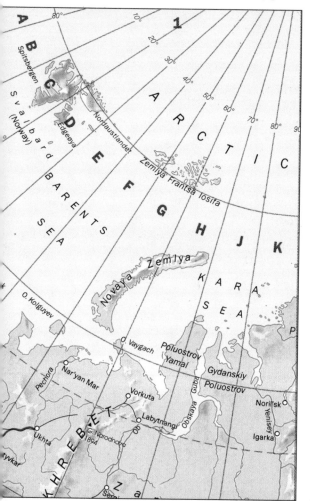

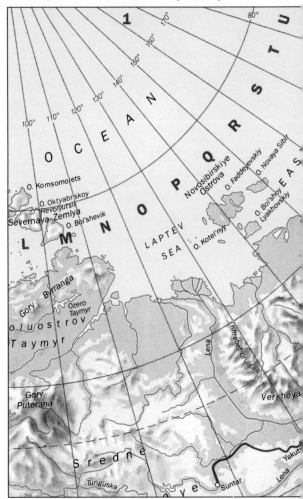

CHUKCHI SEA

Arctic Circle

Chukotskiy Poluostrov

St. Lawrence (U.S.A.)

B E R I N G   S E A

70°

60°

170°

180°

4

CHUKCHI
SEA

Chukotskiy Khrebet

Khrebet Kolymskiy

Koryakskiy Khrebet

K a m c h a t k a

Sredinnyy Khrebet

Zaliv Shelikhova

Magadan

Ust'-Kamchatsk

Klyuchevskaya Sopka
4750

Petropavlovsk-
Kamchatskiy

erskogo

Okhotsk

SEA

OF

OKHOTSK

rebet Dzhugdzhur

Ostrova

rovsk-
skiy
lin

170°

60°

160°

5

3

Sredn

Tunguska

Lena

Suntar

Yak

S i b i r s k o y e

Ploskogorye

S I A

Sta

Yeniseysk   Angara

Skovor

Bratsk

Ozero
Baykal

Krasnoyarsk

Khrebet

Shilka

Tulun

Cheremkhovo

Chita

Yenisey

Vostochnyy Sayan

Angarsk   Irkutsk

Ulan Ude

Borzya

Abakan

Zapadnyy Sayan

Yablonovyy

Manzhouli

Kyzyl

Hövsgöl
Nuur

Choybalsan

Uvs
Nuur

Ulaanbaatar
(Ulan Bator)

Hovd

Tsetserleg

M O N G O L I A

T A I

Altay

Saynshand

G O B I

Hohhot

Baotou

C L H I N A

Lop Nur

Yumen

M

Taiyu

100

110

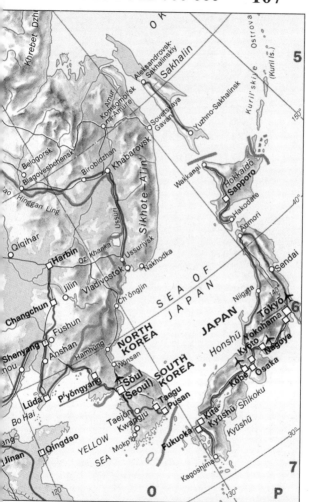

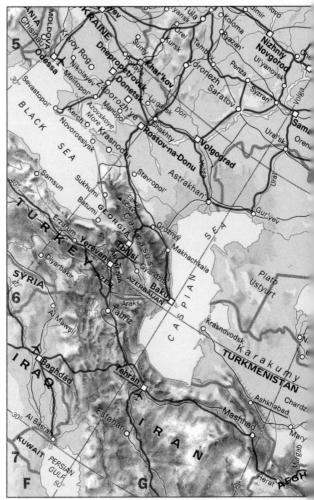

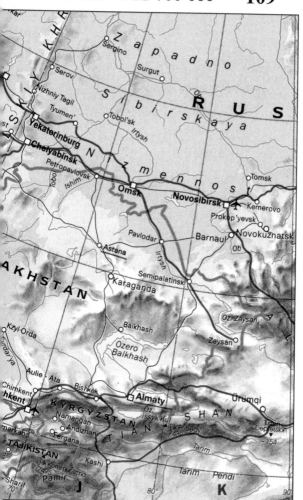

Zapadnyy Sayan
Vostochnyy Sayan
Kyzyl
Cheremkhovo
Angarsk
Irkutsk
Ozero Baykal
Ulan Ude
Uvs Nuur
Hövsgöl Nuur
Selenge
Hangayn Mts.
Onhon
M O N G O L I
Tsetserleg
Ulaanbaatar (Ulan Bator)
Altay
Hami
G O B I
G A N S
Yumen
Qilian Shan
NEI
Baotou
Huang
Qinghai Hu
Yinchuan
Great Wall
olmund
Xining
NINGXIA
NGHAI
Lanzhou
Bayan
Pingliang

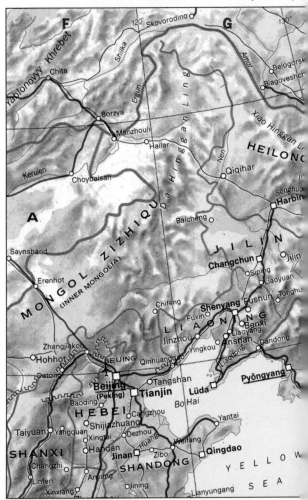

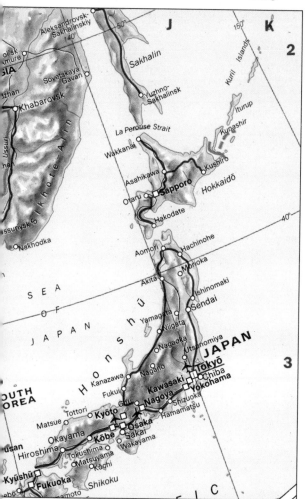

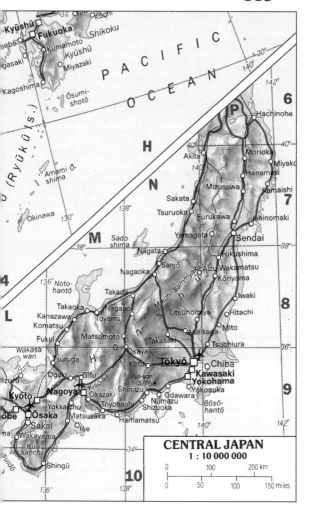

Kyūshū Fukuoka Shikoku Kōchi
sebo Kumamoto Kyūshū
gasaki Miyazaki
Kagoshima Ōsumi-shotō

PACIFIC

OCEAN

(RyūKyū s.) Amami-Ō-shima

Okinawa

P Hachinohe

H Akita Morioka Miyako

N Hanamaki Kamaishi
Mizusawa
Sakata Ishinomaki
M Sado-shima Tsuruoka Furukawa
Yamagata Sendai
Niigata Fukushima
Nagaoka Sanjō Aizu-Wakamatsu
Mkuni-sammyaku Kōriyama
Noto-hantō Takada Iwaki
Takaoka Nagano Utsunomiya Hitachi
Kanazawa Toyama Mito
Komatsu Matsumoto Takasaki Ashikaga Tsuchiura
Fukui Okaya Tōkyō Chiba
Wakasa wan Tsuruga Kōfu Kawasaki
izuru Ogaki Gifu Fuji-san Yokohama
Kyōto Nagoya Okazaki Shimizu Yokosuka
be Yokkaichi Toyohashi Odawara Bōsō-hantō
Ōsaka Matsusaka Numazu Shizuoka
Sakai Ise Hamamatsu
na Wakayama
Kii-sanchi
Shingū

CENTRAL JAPAN
1 : 10 000 000
0   100   200 km
0   50   100   150 miles

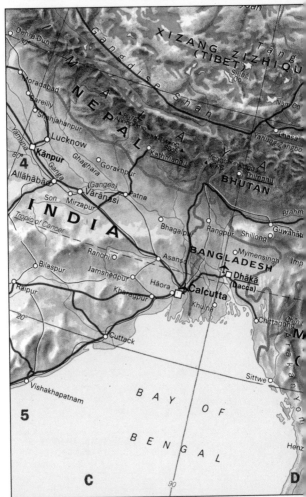

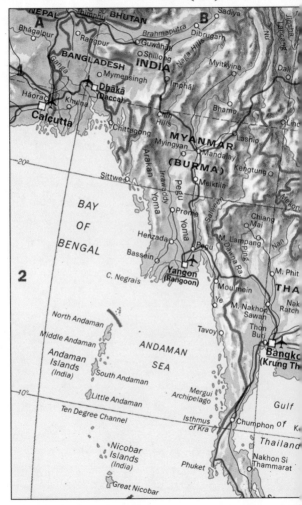

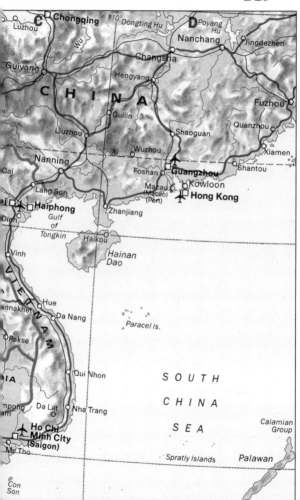

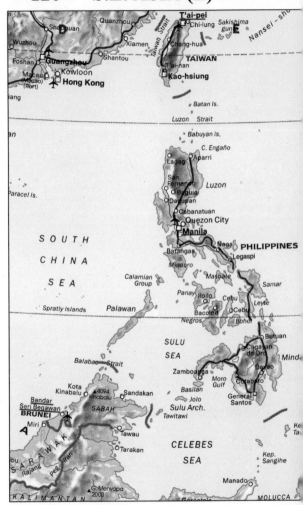

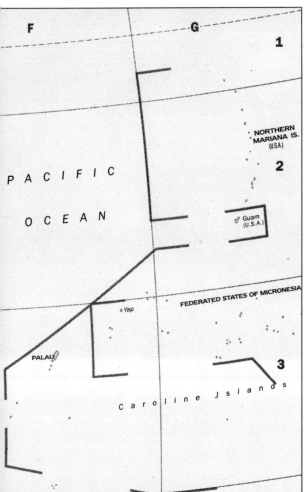

Con
Son

Balabac Strait

Kota
Kinabalu ▲4094
Kinabalu   Sandakan

Bandar
Seri Begawan
BRUNEI   SABAH

L A Y   S   I   Miri

A   Tawau

Natuna
Besar   Tarakan

p. Anambas   Kep.
Natuna
Selatan

Sibu   K
Rajang   A

RE   Singkawang   Kuching   S A R A W A K   Peg. Iran

Pontianak   K A L I M A N T A N   G. Menyapa
2000

Borneo

Samarinda
Balikpapan   Palu

Bangka   Peg. Schwaner

Pangkalpinang   Palangkaraya   Kandangan

ang   Belitung   Makassar   Majene

Tg. Puting   Banjarmasin   Parepare

Laut   Strait

I   N   JAVA SEA   D   O   Ujung
Pandang

betung
Jakarta

jor   Cirebon   Semarang   Madura   FLORES

ndung   G. ▲3428
Slamet   Surakarta   Lesser   Sunda

Yogyakarta   Kediri   **Surabaya**

Malang   Bali   Lombok   Raba

J a w a   (Java)   Banyuwangi

Mataram   Sumbawa

ristmas I.
ustr.)   Sumba

110°   D

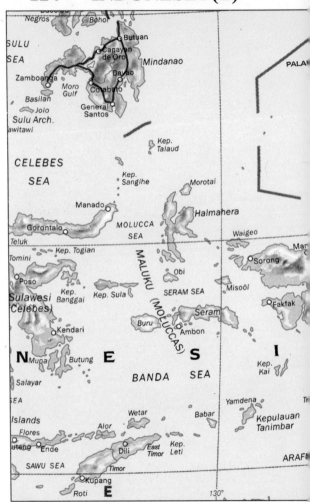

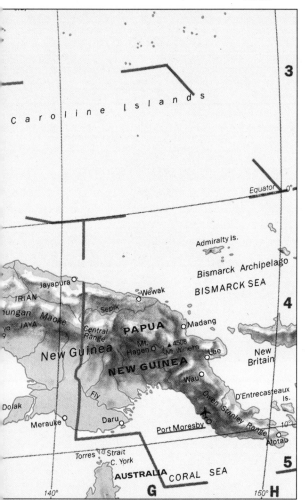

3

C a r o l i n e   I s l a n d s

Equator   0°   **4**

Admiralty Is.

Bismarck Archipelago

BISMARCK SEA

Jayapura

Wewak

IRIAN

Sepik

jungan   Maoke

JAYA   Central
Range   PAPUA   Madang

ya   Mt.   ▲4508
Hagen   Mt. Wilhelm   Lae   New
Britain

New Guinea   **NEW GUINEA**

Wau

Fly   D'Entrecasteaux
Is.

Owen Stanley Range

Dolak

Merauke   Daru   Port Moresby   10°

Alotau   **5**

Torres   Strait
C. York

AUSTRALIA   CORAL SEA

140°   **G**   150°   **H**

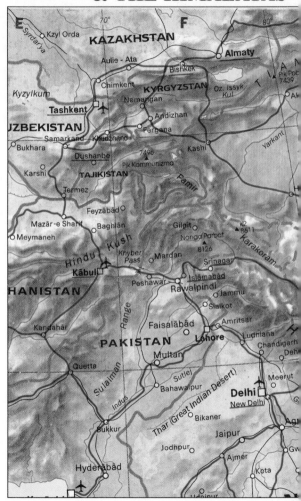

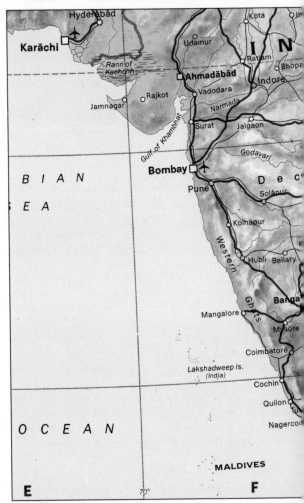

zapur

BANG| **Dhaka**
(Dacca)

A

Asansor

Ranchi
Jamshedpur

Calcutta
Hãora

Kharagpur

Khulna

Chittagong

MYANMAR
(BURMA)

Mandalay

Arakan

Irrawaddy

20°

Cuttack

Sittwe

Yoma

Prome

B A Y

O F

B E N G A L

Bassein

C. Negrais

4

ats
Vishakhapatnam

Kãkinãda

yawada

North Andaman

Middle Andaman

ras

South Andaman
**Andaman
Islands**
(India)

re

alli
lk Str.

Little Andaman

10°

a

Ten Degree Channel

Trincomalee

SRI LANKA

andy

lle

Nicobar Islands
(India)

Great
Nicobar

5

G

90°

H

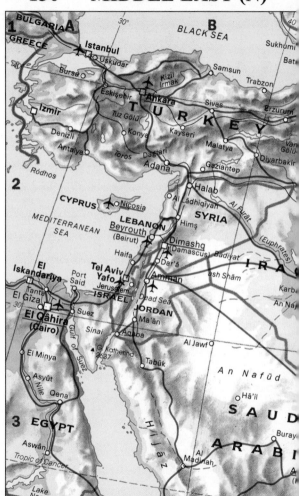

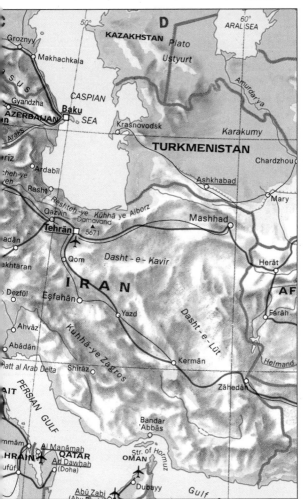

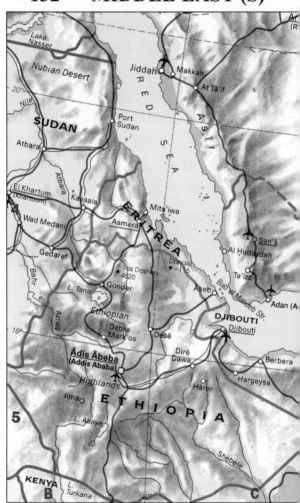

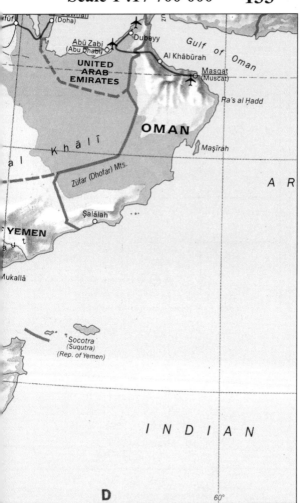

ifūf
o(Doha)

Abū Zabi
(Abu Dhabi) o Dubayy

Gulf of Oman

Al Khābūrah

**UNITED
ARAB
EMIRATES**

Masqat
(Muscat)

Ra's al Ḥadd

OMAN

K h ā l ī

Maṣīrah

a l

A   R

Zŭfar (Dhofar) Mts.

YEMEN
t

Şalālah
o

Mukallā

Socotra
(Suqutra)
(Rep. of Yemen)

I N D I A N

D   60°

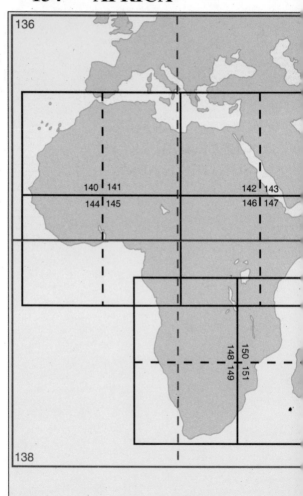

136

140 | 141
144 | 145

142 | 143
146 | 147

148 | 149
150 | 151

138

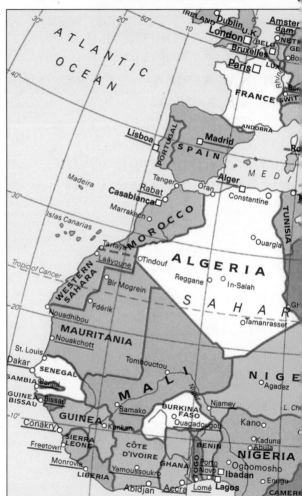

Monrovia
LIBERIA
Yamoussoukro
GHANA
Porto
Novo
Ogbomosho
Ibadan
Enugu
Abidjan
Accra
Lomé **Lagos**
CAMERO
Douala
Yac

Gulf of Guinea
Malabo
Bata
EQUAT.
Libreville
GABO

Príncipe
SÃO TOMÉ &
PRÍNCIPE
São Tomé

0° *Equator*

Annobon

Pointe
Noire
CABINDA
(Angola)

Luanda

Ascension Island
(U.K.)

-10°

Lobit

A T L A N T I C

Namibe

St. Helena
(U.K.)

O C E A N

-20°

Walvis

Tropic of Capricorn

-30°

Tristan da
Cunha
(U.K.)   10°   West of Greenwich 0° East of Greenwich   10°

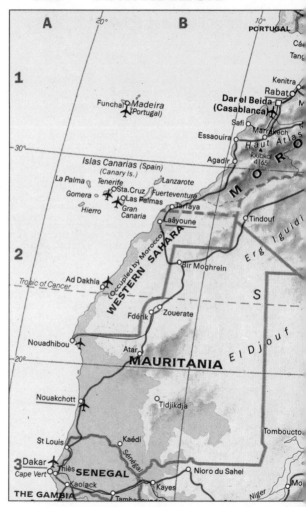

PORTUGAL

Cá
Tang

A   20°   B   10°

1

Kenitra
Rabat

Funchal○Madeira
(Portugal)

**Dar el Beida
(Casablanca)**

Safi

M

Essaouira   ○Marrakech
○ *Haut Atlas*

—30°

Agadir○   Toubkal
4165▲   O

Islas Canarias (Spain)
(Canary Is.)

La Palma○ Tenerife○Lanzarote
Gomera◯◯○Sta.Cruz○Fuerteventura
○Las Palmas
Hierro○   Gran
Canaria   ○Tarfaya

Tindouf

Erg   *Iguidi*

○Laâyoune

2

○Bir Moghrein

Erg   *Iguidi*

Tropic of Cancer   ○Ad Dakhla

S

Occupied by Morocco

WESTERN SAHARA

Fdérik○○Zouerate

El Djouf

Nouadhibou✈

○Atar

—20°

MAURITANIA

Nouakchott✈

○Tidjikdja

Tomboucto

○Kaédi

St Louis○   *Sénégal*

Nioro du Sahel

3 Dakar
Cape Vert✈○Thiès   **SENEGAL**
○Kaolack   ○Kayes   Niger   Mo

THE GAMBIA   Tambacou

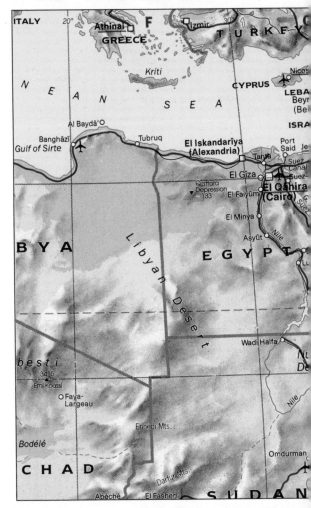

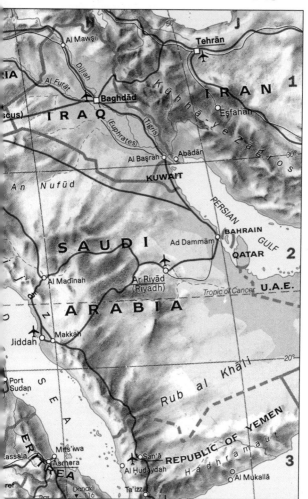

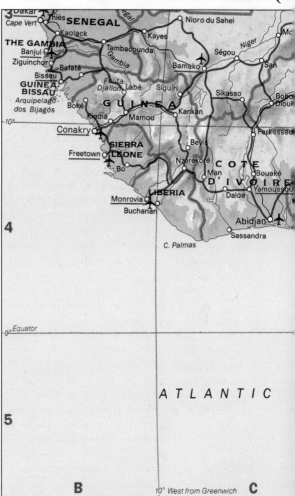

Dakar
Cape Vert
Thiès
SENEGAL
Kaolack
Kayes
Nioro du Sahel
THE GAMBIA
Banjul
Tambacounda
Ségou
Niger
San
Ziguinchor
Bafatá
Gambia
Bamako
Bissau
GUINEA-
BISSAU
Fouta
Djallon
Labé
Siguiri
Sikasso
Bobo
Dioul
Arquipelago
dos Bijagós
Boké
G U I N E A
Kankan
Ferkessé
Kindia
Mamou
Conakry
Beyla
SIERRA
LEONE
Freetown
Nzerekoré
C O T E
Man
Bouaké
Bo
D' I V O I R E
Yamoussou
LIBERIA
Daloa
Monrovia
Buchanan
Abidjan
Sassandra
C. Palmas

ATLANTIC

Equator

10° West from Greenwich

-10º
0°

3
4
5

B
C

Mc

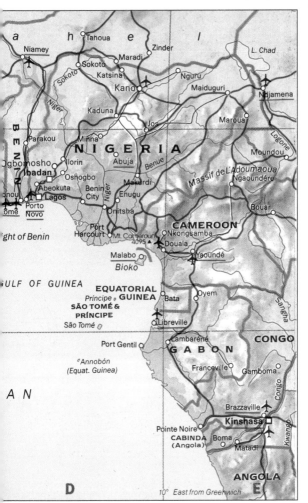

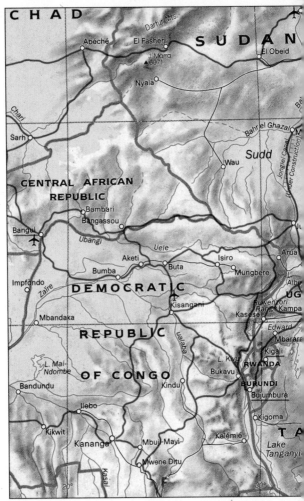

CHAD

Abéché

El Fasher

SUDAN

El Obeid

Darfur Mts.

J. Marra
▲3071

Nyala

Chari

Sarh

Bahr el Ghazal

Wau

Sudd

Jonglei Canal
(under construction)

CENTRAL AFRICAN

REPUBLIC

Bambari

Bangassou

Bangui

Ubangi

Uele

Ju

Arua

Aketi

Buta

Isiro

Bumba

Mungbere

Impfondo

Zaire

DEMOCRATIC

Kisangani

Ruwenzori
Range
Kasese

Kampa

UG

Mbandaka

Ualaba

Edward

Mbarara

REPUBLIC

L. Kivu

Kigali

RWANDA

L. Mai-
Ndombe

Bukavu

BURUNDI

OF CONGO

Kindu

Bujumbura

Bandundu

Ilebo

Kigoma

Kikwit

Kananga

Mbuji-Mayi

Kalémié

TA

Lake
Tanganyi

Mwene Ditu

Kasai

20°

30°

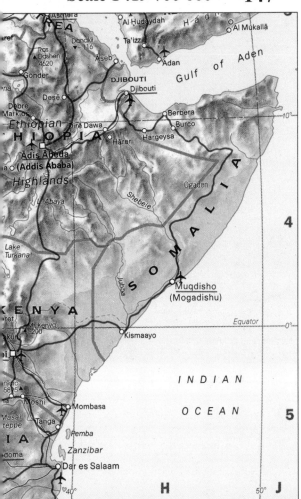

Asmera

~~TEA~~

ref

Ras
Dashen
4620

Gonder

na

Desē

Debre
Mark'os

Ethiopian

H I O P I A

Dirē Dawa

Adis Abeda

a o **(Addis Ababa)**

Highlands

L. Abaya

Shebele

Lake
Turkana

K E N Y A

ret

Mt Kenya
5200

xuru

oi

naro
5895

Moshi

Masai
teppe

Tanga

I A

doma

Al Hudaydah

H a d

Al Mukallā

Ta'izz

Adan

Gulf of Aden

Danakil
▼ ~ 116

Aseb

DJIBOUTI

Djibouti

Berbera

Burco

Hārer

Hargeysa

Ogaden

-10°

S O M A L I A

4

Jubba

Muqdisho
(Mogadishu)

Equator

-0°

Kismaayo

I N D I A N

Mombasa

O C E A N

5

Pemba

Zanzibar

Dar es Salaam

H

40°

50°

J

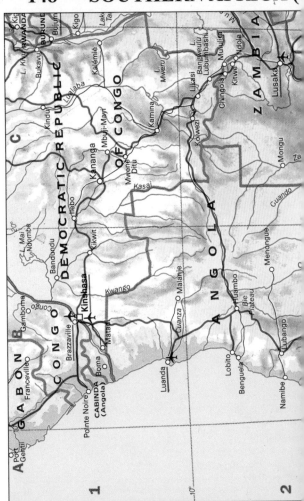

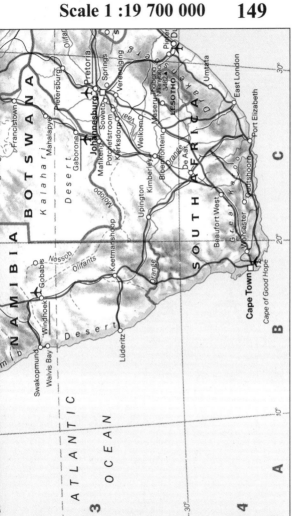

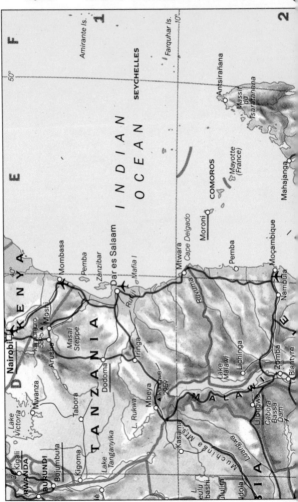

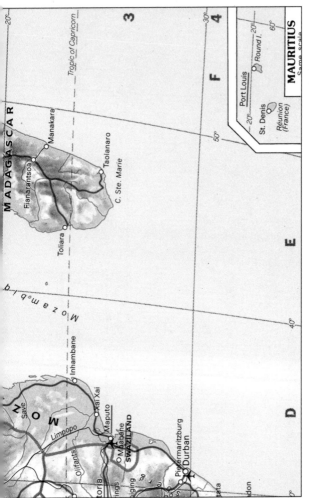

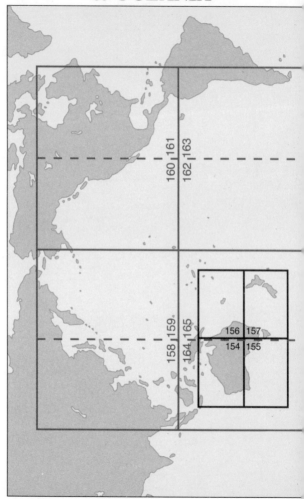

160 161
162 163

158 159
164 165

156 157
154 155

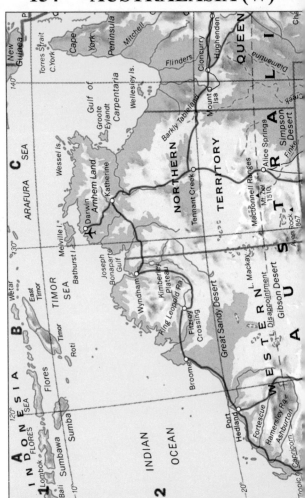

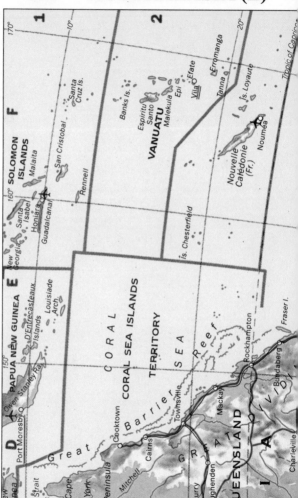

170°

1

10°

2

20°

Tropic of Capricorn

F

Santa Cruz Is.

Banks Is.

Erromango

Vila Efate

Epi

Espiritu Santo

Malekula

Tanna

Îs. Loyauté

SOLOMON ISLANDS

VANUATU

Santa Isabel

Malaita

San Cristobal

Rennell

Nouméa

Nouvelle Calédonie (Fr.)

160°

Honiara

Guadalcanal

New Georgia

E

Îs. Chesterfield

D'Entrecasteaux Islands

Louisiade Arch.

PAPUA NEW GUINEA

150°

C O R A L

CORAL SEA ISLANDS

TERRITORY

S E A

Rockhampton

Fraser I.

Owen Stanley Ra.

Port Moresby

Bundaberg

D

R e e f

G r e a t

B a r r i e r

Townsville

Mackay

Cooktown

Cape York Peninsula

Cairns

Strait

Mitchell

Hughenden

rry

Charleville

QUEENSLAND

G R E A T

D I V I D I N G

I

New nea

East of Greenwich

RUSSIA

☐ Yekaterinburg
Omsk ☐
☐ Novosibirsk
○ Krasnoyarsk
Irkutsk ○
Oz. Baykal
Chita ○

KAZAKHSTAN
○ Astana
○ Karaganda
Oz. Balkhash

MONGOLIA
○ Ulaanbaatar

○ Ürümqi

☐ Almaty

Changchun
Shenyang ☐
Beijing ☐
Tianjin ☐
Jinan ☐ ☐ Lüda
Lanzhou ☐ Qingdao ☐
Xi'an ☐
YELLOW
SEA
Kita
Kyūs

C H I N A Nanjing ☐

Chengdu ☐ Wuhan ☐ Chang Shanghai ☐

Chongqing ☐
EAST
CHINA
SEA
Fuzhou ☐
Ryūkyūs

NEPAL BHUTAN
INDIA
Brahmaputra
BANG.
☐ Dhaka
Calcutta ☐
Irrawaddy
Salween
Mekong

☐ Kunming
Guangzhou ☐
T'ai-pei ☐
TAIWAN

MYANMAR Hanoi ☐
(BURMA)
MACAU Hong Kong

Rangoon ☐
Vientiane ○
Hainan
Dao
Luzon

Andaman Is.
(India)

THAILAND
Bangkok ☐
CAMB.
VIETNAM

☐ Manila

SOUTH Mindoro
PHILIPPINES
Samar

Nicobar Is.
(India)
Phnom ☐
Penh ☐ Ho Chi
Minh City
Gulf of
Thailand
CHINA Palawan
SEA
SULU
SEA Mindanao
PALA

Medan ☐
MALAYSIA
BRUNEI
CELEBES
SEA
○ Kuala
Lumpur

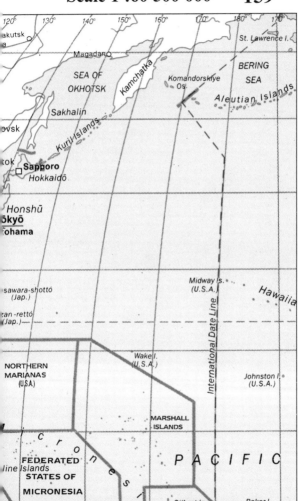

120° 130° 140° 150° 160° 170° 180° 170°

akutsk
a

Magadano

St. Lawrence I.

SEA OF
OKHOTSK

BERING
SEA

Kamchatka

Komandorskiye
Os.

Aleutian Islands

Sakhalin

ovsk

Kuril Islands

tok **Sapporo**
Hokkaidō

Honshū
ōkyō
ohama

sawara-shottó
(Jap.)

Midway Is.
(U.S.A.)

Hawaiia

an-rettó
(Jap.)

NORTHERN
MARIANAS
(U.S.A.)

Wake I.
(U.S.A.)

Johnston I.
(U.S.A.)

International Date Line

c r o n e s i

MARSHALL
ISLANDS

FEDERATED
line Islands
STATES OF
MICRONESIA

P A C I F I C

Gilbert Is.

Baker I.

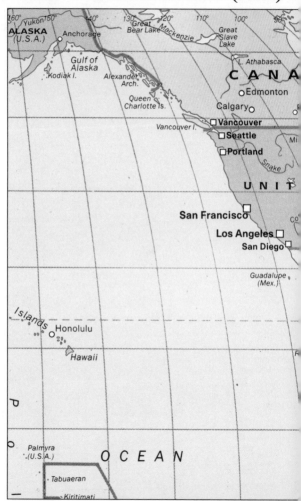

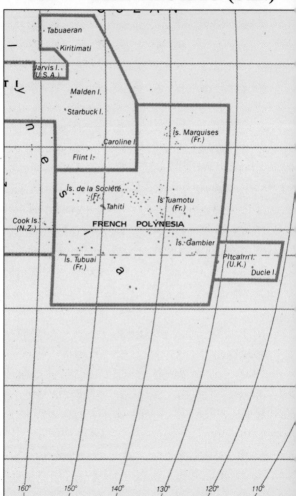

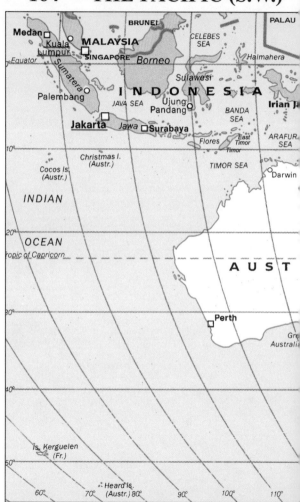

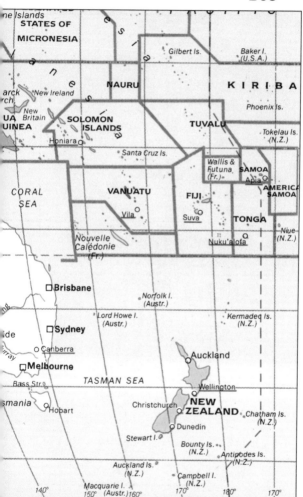

ne Islands
STATES OF MICRONESIA

Gilbert Is.

Baker I.
(U.S.A.)

NAURU

KIRIBA

arck
rch

New Ireland

New
Britain

Phoenix Is.

**UA
UINEA**

**SOLOMON
ISLANDS**

TUVALU

Tokelau Is.
(N.Z.)

Honiara

Santa Cruz Is.

Wallis &
Futuna
(Fr.)

SAMOA

Apia

**CORAL
SEA**

VANUATU

FIJI

**AMERICA
SAMOA**

Vila

Suva

TONGA

Niue
(N.Z.)

Nouvelle
Calédonie
(Fr.)

Nuku'alofa

□**Brisbane**

Norfolk I.
(Austr.)

Lord Howe I.
(Austr.)

Kermadec Is.
(N.Z.)

□**Sydney**

ide

Canberra

□**Melbourne**

TASMAN SEA

Auckland

Wellington

Bass Str.

Christchurch

**NEW
ZEALAND**

Chatham Is.
(N.Z.)

smania

Hobart

Dunedin

Stewart I.

Bounty Is.
(N.Z.)

Antipodes Is.
(N.Z.)

Auckland Is.
(N.Z.)

Campbell I.
(N.Z.)

140°

150°

Macquarie I.
(Austr.)

160°

170°

180°

170°

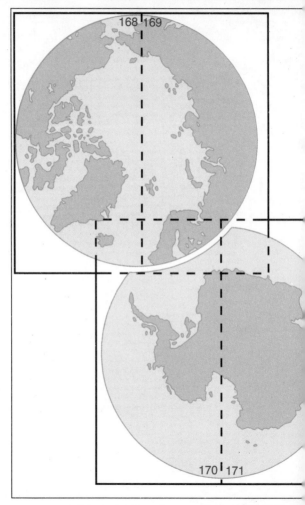

168 169

170 171

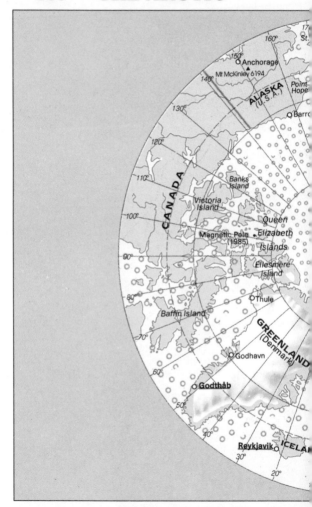

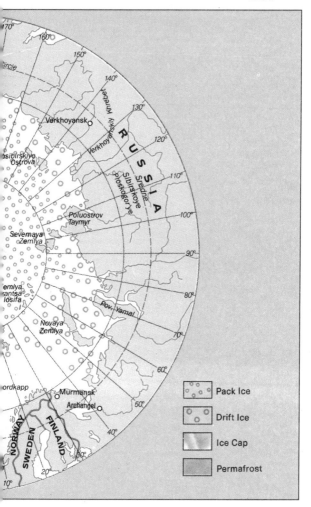

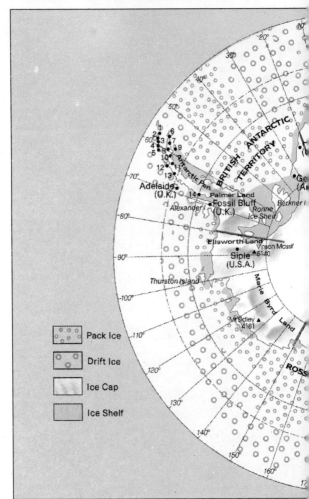

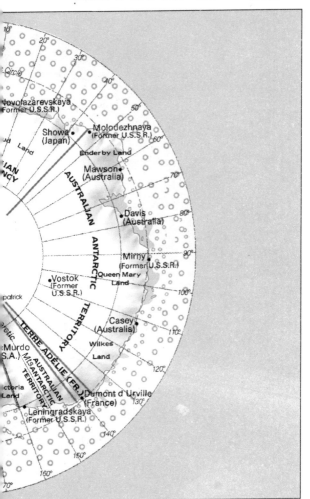

Index

In the index, the first number refers to the page, and the following letter
and number to the section of the map in which the index entry
can be found. For example London 56G6 means that London can
be found on page 56 where column G and row 6 meet.

Abbreviations used in the Index

Afghan	Afghanistan	Fin	Finland	Phil	Phillipines
Alb	Albania	Hung	Hungary	Pol	Poland
Alg	Algeria	Indon.	Indonesia	Port	Portugal
Arg	Argentina	Lat	Latvia	Rep.Yemen	Republic of Yemen
Aust	Australia	Leb	Lebanon	Rom	Romania
Bang	Bangladesh	Lib	Liberia	S.Africa	South Africa
Belg	Belgium	Liech	Liechtenstein	S.Arabia	Saudi Arabia
Bol	Bolivia	Lith	Lithuania	S.Korea	South Korea
Bos.Herz.	Bosnia Herzegovina	Lux	Luxembourg	Scot	Scotland
Bulg	Bulgaria	Madag	Madagascar	Sen	Senegal
Camb	Cambodia	Malay	Malaysia	Slo	Slovenia
Can	Canada	Maur	Mauritania	Switz	Switzerland
CAR	Central African Republic	Mor	Morocco	Tanz	Tanzania
Cro.	Croatia	Mozam	Mozambique	Thai	Thailand
Czech.Rep.	Czech.Republic	N.Ire	Northern Ireland	Turk	Turkey
Dem.Rep.of Congo	Democratic	N.Korea	North Korea	UAE	United Arab Emirates
	Republic of Congo	NZ	New Zealand	UK	United Kingdom
Den	Denmark	Neth	Netherlands	USA	United States of America
Dom Rep.	Dominican Republic	Nic	Nicaragua	Urug	Uruguay
El Sal	El Salvador	Nig	Nigeria	Ven	Venezuela
Eng	England	Nor	Norway	Viet	Vietnam
Eq Guinea	Equatorial Guinea	PNG	Papua New Guinea	Yugos	Yugoslavia
Est	Estonia	Pak	Pakistan	Zim	Zimbabwe
Eth	Ethiopia	Par	Paraguay		
FRG	Federal Republic of Germany				

A

Aachen FRG		90B2
Äänekoski Fin		93F3
Abādān Iran		131C2
Abadla Alg.		141C3
Abakan Rus.		106L4
Abbeville France		68C1
Abéché Chad		146F3
Abeokuta Nig.		145D2
Aberdeen Scot		61F3
Aberfeldy Scot		63E4
Abergavenny Wales		58D6
Abersoch Wales		53C5
Aberystwyth Wales		58C5
Abidjan Côte d'Ivoire		144B2
Aboyne Scot		61F3
Abrantes Port.		72A2
Abū Zabi UAE		133D3
Abuja Nig.		145D2
Acapulco Mexico		23D4
Accra Ghana		145C4
Achill I. Ireland		64A3
Acklins I. The Bahamas		26E2
Acre State Brazil		35B3
Adan Rep.Yemen		132C4
Adana Turk.		130B2
Ad Dakhla Mor.		140B4
Ad Dammām S.Arabia		131D3
Ad Dawhah Qatar		131D3

Adelaide Aust.		155C4
Admiralty Is. Pacific O.		125G4
Agadez Niger		141D5
Agadir Mor.		140C3
Agen France		69C3
Agra India		126F3
Agrigento Italy		79C3
Agropoli Italy		79C2
Aguascalientes Mexico		23C3
Ahmadābād India		128F3
Ahvāz Iran		131C2
Ain Sefra Alg.		141C3
Aizu-Wakamatsu Japan		115N8
Ajaccio Corse		76B2
Ajmer India		126F3
Aketi D		
em. Rep. of Congo		146F4
Akita Japan		115P7
Akmola Kazakhstan		109J4
Akron USA		18E1
Aksu China		126G1
Akureyri Iceland		92B1
Alabama State USA		20E2
Alagoas State Brazil		37F3
Alagoinhas Brazil		37F4
Alajuela Costa Rica		25C5
Åland Is. Fin		95E3
Alaska Pen. USA		12C4
Alaska State. USA		22J
Albacete Spain		75B2

Albany Aust.		155A4
Albany USA		19F1
Al Basrah Iraq		131C2
Al Baydā' Libya		142F1
Alberta State Canada		13G4
Ålborg Den.		94C4
Albuquerque USA		17C2
Albury Aust.		157D4
Alcalá de Henares Spain		72B1
Alcañiz Spain		74B1
Alcázar de San Juan		
Spain		73B2
Alcoy Spain		75B2
Aldan Russia		106O4
Alderney I. UK		59E8
Aldershot Eng.		56G6
Aleksandrovsk-Sakhalinskly		
Russia		107Q4
Alessandria Italy		76B2
Ålesund Nor.		92B3
Aleutian Is. USA		22J
Alexander Arch. USA		23J
Alexander I. Ant.		P170
Alexandria Egypt		142F1
Alexandroúpolis Greece		81F2
Algeciras Spain		73A2
Alger Alg.		141D3
Alicante Spain		75B2
Alice Springs Aust.		154C3
Allhābād India		127G3

Al Hudaydah Rep.Yemen	132C4
Al Hufūf S.Arabia	131C3
Al Jawf S.Arabia	130B3
Al Khāburah Oman	133D3
Al Kuwayt Kuwait	131C3
Al Lādhiqīyah Syria	130B2
Al Madinah S.Arabia	130B3
Almada Port.	73A2
Almaty Kazakhstan	109J5
Al Manāmah Bahrain	131D3
Al Mawsil Iraq	130C2
Al Mukallā Rep. Yemen	133C4
Almeria Spain	75B2
Alnwick Eng	54F2
Alorī. Indon.	124E4
Alotau PNG	125H5
Alta Nor.	93E2
Altay Mongolia	111D2
Amami Ō-shima I. Japan	115G4
Amapá State Brazil	36D2
Amarillo USA	17C2
Amazonas State Brazil	35C3
Ambon Indon.	124E4
Amfilokhía Greece	80E3
Amiens France	68C2
Amirante Is. Indian O.	150F1
Amman Jordan	130B2
Amorgós I. Greece	81F3
Ampia Western Samoa	165
Amposta Spain	74C1
Amritsar India	126F2
Amsterdam Neth.	84A2
An Najaf Iraq	130C2
An Uaimh Ireland	67E3
Anáfi I. Greece	81F3
Anápolis Brazil	37E4
Anchorage USA	12D3
Ancona Italy	77C2
Andalucia Region Spain	73A2
Andaman Islands India	129H4
Andizhan Uzbekistan	109J5
Andorra la Vella Andorra	74C1
Andorra, Principality SW Europe	74C1
Andros I. Bahamas	24D2
Ándros Greece	81E3
Angarsk Rus	106M4
Angers France	68B2
Anglesey I. Wales	53C3
Angoulême France	69C2
Anguilla I. Caribbean Sea	26G3
Anhui Province China	114F3
Anjou Province France	68B2
Ankara Turk.	130B2
'Annaba Alg.	141D3
Annapolis USA	18F2
Annecy France	71D2
Annobón I. Eq.Guinea	145D3
Anqing China	114F3
Anshan China	112G2
Anshun China	117E4
Antalya Turk.	130B2
Antananarivo Madag.	151E2
Antarctic Circle Ant.	P170
Antequera Spain	73B2
Anticosti I. Canada	15M5

Antigua I. Leeward Is.	26G3
Antipodes Is. NZ	165
Antofagasta Chile	40B5
Antrim N.Ire.	65E2
Antsirabe Madag.	151E2
Antsiranana Madag.	150E2
Antwerpen Belg.	70C1
Anyang China	112F3
Aomori Japan	113J2
Aosta Italy	76B1
Aparri Phil.	120E2
Apatity Rus	93G2
Apeldoorn Neth.	84B2
Appleby-in-Westmorland Eng	53E3
Aqaba Jordan	130B3
Ar Riyāδ S.Arabia	130C3
Aracaju Brazil	37F4
Aracena Spain	73A2
Arad Rom.	88E3
Aran I. Ireland	64C1
Aran Is. Ireland	66B3
Aranda de Duero Spain	72B1
Arbatax Sardegna	78B3
Arbroath Scot	63F4
Arcachon France	69B3
Arch de los Chonos Chile	41B7
Archangel Rus	102F3
Ardabīl Iran	131C2
Ardara Ireland	64C2
Arendal Nor.	94B4
Arequipa Peru	35B4
Arezzo Italy	77C2
Argenton-S-Creuse France	69C2
Argos Greece	80E3
Århus Den.	94C4
Arica Chile	35B4
Arisaig Scot	62C4
Arizona State USA	16B2
Arkansas State USA	18D2
Arklow Ireland	67E4
Arles France	71C3
Armagh N.Ire.	65E2
Arnhem Neth.	84B2
Arran I. Scot	62C5
Arrochar Scot	62D4
Árta Greece	80E3
Artois Province France	68C1
Arua Uganda	146G4
Aruba I. Caribbean Sea	27F4
Arusha Tanz.	147G5
Arvida Canada	15L5
Arvika Sweden	94C4
Asahikawa Japan	113J2
Asansol India	129G3
Āseb Eth.	147H3
Ashford Eng	56H6
Ashikaga Japan	115N8
Ashington Eng	54F2
Ashkhabad Turkmenistan	108G6
Asmera Eritrea.	143G3
Astipálaia I. Greece	81F3
Astrakhan' Rus	108F5
Asturias Region Spain	72A1
Asunción Par.	38E5
Aswān Egypt	142G2
Asyūt Egypt	142G2

At. Martin's Isles of Scilly	59A8
At Tā'if S.Arabia	132C3
Atar Maur.	140B4
Atbara Sudan	142G3
Athenry Ireland	66C3
Athens Greece	81E3
Athinaí Greece	81E3
Athlone Ireland	66D3
Atlanta USA	18E2
Atyrau Kazakhstan	108G5
Auckland NZ	157G4
Auckland Is. NZ	165
Augsburg FRG	91C3
Augusta Aust.	155A4
Augusta Georgia USA	18E2
Augusta Maine USA	19G1
Augustow Pol.	86E2
Aulie-Ata Kazakhstan	109J5
Austin USA	23D2
Auvergne Province France	71C2
Auxerre France	70C2
Aveiro Port.	72A1
Avellino Italy	79C2
Avesta Sweden	94D3
Avezzano Italy	77C2
Aviemore Scot	61E3
Avignon France	71C3
Avila Spain	74B1
Avilés Spain	72A1
Axel Heiberg I. Canada	14J2
Axminster Eng	59E7
Áyios Evstrátios I. Greece	81F3
Aylesbury Eng	56G6
Ayr Scot	62D5
Az Zawiyah Libya	141E3

B

Babar I. Indon.	124E4
Babuyan I. Phil.	120E2
Bacau Rom.	89F3
Bacolod Phil.	120E2
Badajoz Spain	73A2
Badalona Spain	74C1
Bafatá Guinea-Bissau	144A1
Baffin Island Canada	14K2
Bagé Brazil	38E6
Baghdād Iraq	130C2
Baghlān Afghan.	126E2
Baguio Phil.	120E2
Bahamas Is.,The, Caribbean	26E1
Bahawalpur Pak.	126F3
Bahía Blanca Arg.	40C6
Bahia State Brazil	37E4
Baia Mare Rom.	88E3
Baicheng China	112K2
Baker I. Pacific O.	165
Bakhtaran Iran	131C2
Baku Azerbaijan	108F5
Bala Wales	53D5
Balbriggan Ireland	67E3
Balearic Is. Spain	74C2
Bali I. Indon.	123D4
Balikpapan Indon.	123D4
Balkhash Kazakhstan	109J5
Ballachulish Scot	62C4
Ballantrae Scot	62D5
Ballarat Aust.	157D4

Ballina *Ireland*	64B2	Bayonne *France*	69B3	Bîrlad *Rom.*	89F3
Ballinasloe *Ireland*	66C3	Bayreuth *FRG*	91C3	Birmingham *Eng*	56F5
Ballygawley *N.Ire.*	65D2	Baza *Spain*	73B2	Birmingham *USA*	18E2
Ballymena *N.Ire.*	65E2	Beaufort West *S.Africa*	149C4	Birobidzhan *Russia*	107P5
Baltimore *USA*	19F2	Beauly *Scot*	60D3	Birr *Ireland*	66D3
Bamako *Mali*	144B1	Beauvais *France*	68C2	Bishkek *Kyrgyztan*	109J5
Bambari *CAR*	146F4	Béchar *Alg.*	141C3	Bishop Auckland *Eng*	54F3
Bamberg *FRG*	91C3	Bedford *Eng*	56G5	Biskra *Alg.*	141D3
Banda Aceh *Indon.*	122B3	Beijing *China*	112F3	Bismarck *USA*	17C1
Bandar 'Abbās *Iran*	131D3	Beijing Province *China*	112F3	Bismarck Arch. *Pacific O.*	125H4
Bandar Seri Begawan		Beira *Mozam.*	151D2	Bissau *Guinea-Bissau*	144A1
Brunei	123D3	Beja *Port.*	73A2	Bitola *Yugos.*	80E2
Bandon *Ireland*	66C5	Béjar *Spain*	72A1	Bizerte *Tunisia*	141D3
Bandundu		Belcher Is. *Canada*	15K4	Blace *Cro.*	82D2
Dem. Rep. of Congo	146E5	Belcoo *N.Ire.*	64D2	Blackburn *Eng*	53E4
Banff *Scot*	61F3	Belém *Brazil*	36E2	Blackpool *Eng*	53D4
Bangalore *India*	128F5	Belfast *N.Ire.*	65F2	Blagævgrad *Bulg.*	82E2
Bangassou *CAR*	146F4	Belfort *France*	70D2	Blagoveshchensk *Russia*	107O4
Banghāzi *Libya*	142F1	Belgrade *Yugos.*	82E2	Blair Atholl *Scot*	62E4
Bangka I. *Indon.*	123C4	Belhai *China*	117E4	Blantyre *Malawi*	150D2
Bangkok *Thai.*	118C2	Belitung *Indon.*	123C4	Blida *Alg.*	141D3
Bangor *N.Ire.*	65F2	Belize *Belize*	24B3	Bloemfontein *S.Africa*	149C3
Bangor *Wales*	53C4	Bellary *India*	128F4	Blönduós *Iceland*	92A1
Bangui *CAR*	146E4	Belle Ile *France*	68B2	Bluefields *Nic.*	25C4
Banja Luka *Bos. Herz.*	77D2	Bello *Colombia*	34B2	Blyth *Eng*	54F2
Banjarmasin *Indon.*	123D4	Belmullet *Ireland*	64A2	Bo *Sierra Leone*	144A2
Banjul *The Gambia*	140B5	Belo Horizonte *Brazil*	37E4	Boa Vista *Brazil*	34C2
Bank Is. *Vanuatu*	156F2	Belogorsk *Rus*	107O4	Bobo Dioulasso	
Banks I. *Canada*	12F2	Belopan *Guatemala*	24B3	*Burkina Faso*	144B1
Bantry *Ireland*	66B5	Benavente *Spain*	72A1	Bocas del Toro *Panama*	25C5
Banyuwangi *Indon.*	123D4	Benbecula I. *Scot*	60A3	Boden *Sweden*	93E2
Baoding *China*	112F3	Bendigo *Aust.*	157D4	Bodmin *Eng*	59C7
Baoji *China*	117E3	Benevento *Italy*	79C2	Bodø *Nor.*	92C2
Baotou *China*	111E2	Bengbu *China*	114F3	Bodrum *Turkey*	81F3
Baracaldo *Spain*	72B1	Benguela *Angola*	148B2	Bognor Regis *Eng*	57G7
Barbados I. *Caribbean Is.*	27H4	Benicarló *Spain*	74C1	Bogor *Indon.*	123C4
Barbuda I. *Leeward Is.*	26G3	Benidorm *Spain*	75B2	Bogotá *Colombia*	34B2
Barcelona *Spain*	74C1	Benin City *Nig.*	145D2	Bohol *Phil.*	120E3
Barcelona *Ven.*	34C1	Benxi *China*	112G2	Boise *USA*	16B1
Bareilly *India*	126F3	Berat *Alb.*	80D2	Boké *Guinea*	144A1
Bari *Italy*	79D2	Berbera *Somalia*	147H3	Bollnäs *Sweden*	94D3
Barletta *Italy*	79D2	Bergamo *Italy*	76B1	Bologna *Italy*	77C2
Barnaul *Russia*	109K4	Bergen *Nor.*	94B3	Bolton *Eng*	53E4
Barnstaple *Eng*	58C6	Berkner I. *Ant.*	P170	Boma	
Barquisimeto *Ven.*	34C1	Berlin *FRG*	85C2	*Dem. Rep. of Congo*	145E3
Barra I. *Scot*	60A3	Bermuda I. *Atlantic O.*	19G2	Bombay (Mumbai) *India*	124E4
Barranquilla *Colombia*	34B1	Bern *Switz.*	70D2	Bonaire *Caribbean Sea*	27F4
Barrow *USA*	12C2	Berry Province *France*	68C2	Bonn *FRG*	90B2
Barrow-in-Furness *Eng*	53D3	Berwick-upon-Tweed *Eng*	54F2	Boothia Pen. *Canada*	14J2
Barry *Wales*	58D6	Besançon *France*	70D2	Borås *Sweden*	94C4
Basel *Switz.*	70D2	Betanzos *Spain*	72A1	Bordeaux *France*	69B3
Basilan I. *Phil.*	120E3	Beverley *Eng*	55G4	Borneo *Indon./Malay.*	123D3
Basildon *Eng*	56H6	Beyla *Guinea*	144B2	Bornholm I. *Den.*	94C4
Basingstoke *Eng*	56F6	Beyrouth *Leb.*	130B2	Borzya *Russia*	106N4
Bassein *Myanmar*	118B2	Béziers *France*	71C3	Bosanski Brod *Cro.*	82D1
Bastia *Corse*	76B2	Bhagalpur *India*	127G3	Boston *Eng*	55G5
Bata *Eq. Guinea*	145D2	Bhamo *Myanmar*	118B1	Boston *Eng*	55G5
Batan I. *Phil.*	120E1	Bhopal *India*	128F3	Boston *USA*	19F1
Batang *China*	117D3	Biak I. *Indon.*	125F4	Bouaké *Côte d'Ivoire*	144B2
Batangas *Phil.*	120E2	Bialystok *Pol.*	86E2	Bouar *CAR*	145E2
Bath *Eng*	58E6	Bideford *Eng*	58C6	Bouârfa *Mor.*	141C3
Bathurst I. *Aust.*	154B2	Biel *Switz.*	70D2	Boulogne *France*	68C1
Bathurst I. *Canada*	12H2	Bikaner *India*	126F3	Bounty Is. *NZ*	165
Batley *Eng*	55F4	Bilaspur *India*	129G3	Bourg-en-Bresse *France*	71D2
Battambang *Camb.*	118C2	Billings *USA*	17C1	Bourges *France*	68C2
Batumi *Georgia*	108F5	Bioko I. *Atlantic O.*	145D2	Bourgogne Province *France*	70C2
		Bir Moghrein *Maur.*	140B4	Bournemouth *Eng*	57F7
Bayeaux *France*	68B2	Birkenhead *Eng*	53D4	Boyle *Ireland*	64C3
				Brač I. *Yugos.*	77D2
				Bräcke *Sweden*	92D3

Bradford *Eng*	55F4
Braga *Port.*	72A1
Braila *Rom.*	89F3
Brasília *Brazil*	37E4
Brasov *Rom.*	89F3
Bratislava *Slovakia*	88D3
Bratsk *Russia*	106M4
Braunschweig *FRG*	85C2
Bray *Ireland*	67E3
Brazzaville *Congo*	145E3
Breda *Neth.*	84A2
Bremen *FRG*	84B2
Bremerhaven *FRG*	84B2
Brescia *Italy*	76C1
Bressay *Scot*	61J7
Bressuire *France*	68B2
Brest *Belarus*	102D4
Brest *France*	68B2
Bretagne Province *France*	68B2
Briançon *France*	71D3
Briare *France*	70C2
Bridgetown *Barbados*	27H4
Bridgwater *Eng*	58D6
Bridlington *Eng*	55G3
Brighton *Eng*	57G7
Brindisi *Italy*	79D2
Brisbane *Aust.*	156E3
Bristol *Eng*	58E6
British Columbia State *Canada*	13F4
Brive-la-Gaillarde *France*	69C2
Brno *Czech.*	91D3
Broken Hill *Aust.*	155E4
Broome *Aust.*	154B2
Brora *Scot*	61E2
Brownsville *USA*	23D3
Bruck an der Mur *Aust.*	91D3
Brunei, Sultanate *SE Asia*	123D3
Brussels *Belg.*	70C1
Bruxelles *Belg.*	70C1
Bryansk *Russia*	102E4
Bucaramanga *Colombia*	34B2
Buchanan *Lib.*	144A2
Bucharest *Rom.*	83F2
Buckie *Scot*	61F3
Buckingham *Eng*	56F6
Budapest *Hung.*	88D3
Bude *Eng*	59C7
Buenaventura *Colombia*	34B2
Buenos Aires *Arg.*	40D6
Buenos Aires State *Arg.*	38D6
Buffalo *USA*	17C1
Buffalo *USA*	18F1
Builth Wells *Wales*	58D5
Bujumbura *Burundi*	146F5
Bukavu *Dem.Rep.of Congo*	146F5
Bukhara *Uzbekistan*	108H6
Bukittinggi *Indon.*	122C4
Bulawayo *Zim.*	155A4
Bumba *Dem.Rep. of Congo*	146F4
Bunbury *Aust.*	154A4
Bundaberg *Aust.*	156E3
Bundoran *Ireland*	64C2
Buraydah *S.Arabia*	130C3
Burco *Somalia*	147H4
Burgas *Bulg.*	83F2
Burgos *Spain*	72B1
Burley *USA*	17B1
Bursa *Turk.*	130A1
Buru I. *Indon.*	124E4
Bury St. Edmunds *Eng*	56H5
Buta *Dem.Rep. of Congo*	146F4
Bute *Scot*	62C5
Butte *USA*	17B1
Butuan *Phil.*	120E3
Butung I. *Indon.*	124E4
Buzau *Rom.*	89F3
Byala *Bulg.*	83F2
Bydgoszcz *Pol.*	86D2
Bylot I. *Canada*	14L2
Bytom *Pol.*	88D2

C

Cabanatuan *Phil.*	120E2
Cabimas *Ven.*	34B1
Cabinda *Angola*	145E3
Cacak *Yugos.*	82E2
Cáceres *Spain*	73A2
Cádiz *Spain*	73A2
Caen *France*	68B2
Caernarfon *Wales*	53C4
Cagayan de Oro *Phil.*	120E3
Cagliari *Sardegna*	78B3
Caher *Ireland*	66D4
Cahors *France*	69C3
Caicos Is. *Caribbean Sea*	26E2
Cairns *Aust.*	156D2
Cairo *Egypt*	142G1
Calahorra *Spain*	74B1
Calais *France*	68C1
Calama *Chile*	40B5
Calamian Group *Phil.*	120D2
Calatayud *Spain*	74B1
Calcutta *India*	129G3
Cali *Colombia*	34B2
California State *USA*	16A2
Callao *Peru*	35B4
Calvi *Corse*	76B2
Camagüey *Cuba*	24D2
Cambeltown *Scot*	62C5
Cambridge *Eng*	56H5
Camden *USA*	19F2
Campbell I. *NZ*	165
Campinas *Brazil*	38F5
Campo Grande *Brazil*	37D5
Campos *Brazil*	38F5
Can Tho *Viet.*	119C2
Canberra *Aust.*	157D4
Cangziou *China*	112F3
Cannes *France*	71D3
Canterbury *Eng*	56J6
Cap-Haïtien *Haiti*	26E3
Cape Breton I. *Canada*	15M5
Cape Town *S.Africa*	149B4
Capri I. *Italy*	79C2
Caracal *Rom.*	83E2
Caracaraí *Brazil*	34C2
Caracas *Ven.*	34C1
Caransebes *Rom.*	88E3
Carbonia *Sardegna*	78B3
Carcassonne *France*	69C3
Cardiff *Wales*	58D6
Cardigan *Wales*	58C5
Carlisle *Eng*	52E3
Carlow *Ireland*	67E4
Carmarthen *Wales*	58C6
Carnarvon *Aust.*	154A3

Carolina *Brazil*	37E3
Caroline I. *Kiribati*	162
Caroline Is. *Pacific O.*	125G3
Carrick on Shannon *Ireland*	64C3
Carrickmacross *Ireland*	65E3
Carson City *USA*	16B2
Cartagena *Colombia*	34B1
Cartagena *Spain*	75B2
Cartago *Costa Rica*	25C5
Caserta *Italy*	79C2
Cashel *Ireland*	67D4
Casper *USA*	17C1
Cassino *Italy*	79C2
Castellón de la Plana *Spain*	74B2
Castilla La Mancha Region *Spain*	73B2
Castilla y León Region *Spain*	72A1
Castlebar *Ireland*	64B3
Castleford *Eng*	55F4
Castries *St. Lucia*	27G4
Castrovillari *Italy*	79D3
Cat Island *The Bahamas*	26D1
Cataluña Region *Spain*	74C1
Catamarca State *Arg.*	40C5
Catania *Italy*	79D3
Catanzaro *Italy*	79D3
Catereggio *Corse*	76B2
Cavan *Ireland*	65D3
Cayenne *French Guiana*	36D2
Cayman Islands *Caribbean Sea*	24C3
Ceará State *Brazil*	37F3
Cebu I. *Phil.*	120E2
Cebu *Phil.*	120E2
Cecina *Italy*	76C2
Cefalù *Italy*	79C3
Cerignola *Italy*	79D2
Ceské Budejovice *Czech. Rep*	91C3
Ceuta *Spain*	73A2
Ch'ongjin *N.Korea*	113G2
Chaco State *Arg.*	40C5
Chalon-sur-Saône *France*	71D2
Châlons-sur-Marne *France*	70C2
Chambéry *France*	71D2
Champagne Province *France*	70C2
Chañaral *Chile*	40B5
Chandigarh *India*	126F2
Chang-hua *Taiwan*	120E1
Changchun *China*	112G2
Changde *China*	114F4
Changsha *China*	114F4
Changzhi *China*	112F3
Channel Is. *UK*	59E8
Channel Port-aux-Basques *Canada*	15N5
Chardzhou *Turkmenistan*	108H6
Charleroi *Belg.*	70C1
Charleston *USA*	18F2
Charleville *Aust.*	156D3
Charlotte *USA*	18E2
Charlottetown *Canada*	15M5
Chartres *France*	68C2
Châteauroux *France*	69C2
Chatham Is. *NZ*	165
Chattanooga *USA*	18E2
Chaumont *France*	70D2
Chaves *Port.*	72A1

Cheboksary *Russia*	108F4
Cheju do I. *S.Korea*	114G3
Chelmsford *Eng*	56H6
Cheltenham *Eng*	59E6
Chelyabinsk *Russia*	109H4
Chemnitz *FRG*	91C2
Chen Xian *China*	114F4
Chengdu *China*	117E3
Chennai (Madras) *India*	129G4
Cherbourg *France*	68B2
Cheremkhovo *Russia*	106M4
Cherepovets *Russia*	102E4
Chernigov *Ukraine*	102E4
Chernovtsy *Ukraine*	102D5
Chesham *Eng*	56G6
Chester *Eng*	53E4
Chesterfield Inlet *Canada*	14J3
Chetumal *Mexico*	24B3
Cheyenne *USA*	17C1
Chiang Mai *Thai.*	118B2
Chiba *Japan*	115P9
Chicago *USA*	18E1
Chichester *Eng*	57G7
Chiclayo *Peru*	35B3
Chifeng *China*	112F2
Chihuahua *Mexico*	23C3
Chi-lung *Taiwan*	120E1
Chimbote *Peru*	35B3
Chimkent *Kazakhstan*	109H5
Chingola *Zambia*	148C2
Chippenham *Eng*	56E6
Chisinau *Moldova*	108D5
Chita *Russia*	106N4
Chittagong *Bang.*	129H3
Chojnice *Pol.*	85D2
Chongqing *China*	117E4
Chorley *Eng*	53E4
Choybalsan *Mongolia*	112F2
Christchurch *NZ*	157G5
Christmas I. *Indian O.*	123C5
Chubut State *Arg.*	41C2
Chumphon *Thai.*	118B2
Church Stretton *Eng*	58E5
Churchill *Canada*	15J4
Cienfuegos *Cuba*	24C2
Cieza *Spain*	75B2
Cîmpina *Rom.*	89F3
Cincinnati *USA*	18E2
Cirebon *Indon.*	123C4
Citta di Castello *Italy*	77C2
Ciudad Bolivar *Ven.*	34C2
Ciudad Guayana *Ven.*	34C2
Ciudad Juárez *Mexico*	23C2
Ciudad Real *Spain*	73B2
Ciudad Rodrigo *Spain*	72A1
Civitanova Marche *Italy*	77C2
Civitavecchia *Italy*	77C2
Clacton-on-Sea *Eng*	56J6
Clare I. *Ireland*	64A3
Claremorris *Ireland*	66B3
Clermont Ferrand *France*	71C2
Cleveland *USA*	18E1
Clifden *Ireland*	66A3
Cloghan *Ireland*	66D3
Cloncurry *Aust.*	154D2
Clonmel *Ireland*	67D4
Cluj-Napoca *Rom.*	88E3
Coatbridge *Scot*	63D5
Cobán *Guatemala*	25A3
Cobh *Ireland*	66C5
Cochabamba *Bolivia*	35C4
Cochin *India*	128F5
Cocos I. *Indian O.*	122B5
Codó *Brazil*	37E3
Coimbatore *India*	128F4
Coimbra *Port.*	72A1
Colchester *Eng*	56H6
Coleraine *N.Ire.*	65E1
Coll I. *Scot*	62B4
Collooney *Ireland*	64C2
Colmar *France*	70D2
Colombo *Sri Lanka*	129F5
Colombus *USA*	18E2
Colón *Panama*	25D5
Colonsay I. *Scot*	62B4
Colorado Springs *USA*	17C2
Colorado State *USA*	17C2
Columbia *USA*	18E2
Columbus *USA*	20E2
Como *Italy*	76B1
Comodoro Rivadavia *Arg.*	41C7
Comoros Is. *Indian O.*	150E2
Compiègne *France*	70C2
Conakry *Guinea*	144A2
Concepción *Chile*	40B6
Concepción *Par.*	38E5
Concord *USA*	19F1
Concordia *Arg.*	38E6
Connecticut State *USA*	19F1
Consett *Eng*	54F3
Constanta *Rom.*	83F2
Constantine *Alg.*	141D3
Contonou *Benin*	145D2
Cook Is. *Pacific O.*	162
Cooktown *Aust.*	156D2
Copenhagen *Den.*	94C4
Corby *Eng*	56G5
Corcubion *Spain*	72A1
Córdoba *Arg.*	40C6
Córdoba *Spain*	73B2
Cordoba State *Arg.*	40C6
Corfu I. *Greece*	80D3
Corigliano *Italy*	79D3
Corinto *Nic.*	25B4
Cork *Ireland*	66C5
Coro *Ven.*	34C1
Corpus Christi *USA*	23D3
Corrientes *Arg.*	40D5
Corrientes State *Arg.*	38E5
Corse I. *France*	76B2
Corumbá *Brazil*	37D4
Cosenza *Italy*	79D3
Cospic *Cro.*	77D2
Cotabato *Phil.*	120E3
Cottbus *FRG*	85C2
Coventry *Eng*	56F5
Cowes *Isle of Wight*	57F7
Craiova *Rom.*	82E2
Crawley *Eng*	56G6
Cres I. *Cro.*	77C2
Crete I. *Greece*	81E3
Crewe *Eng*	53E4
Crianlarich *Scot*	62D4
Crieff *Scot*	62E4
Cromer *Eng*	55J5
Crotone *Italy*	79D3
Cruzeiro do Sul *Brazil*	35B3
Cucui *Brazil*	34C2
Cúcuta *Colombia*	34B2
Cuddalore *India*	129F4
Cuenca *Ecuador*	35B3
Cuenca *Spain*	74B1
Cuiabá *Brazil*	37D4
Culiacán *Mexico*	23C3
Cumbernauld *Scot*	63D5
Cumnock *Scot*	62D5
Cuneo *Italy*	76B2
Cupar *Scot*	63E4
Curaçao *Caribbean Sea*	27F4
Curitiba *Brazil*	38F5
Cuttack *India*	129G3
Cuxhaven *FRG*	84B2
Cuzco *Peru*	35B4
Cwmbran *Wales*	58D6
Cyprus *Med.Sea*	130B2
Czestochowa *Pol.*	88D2

D

Dagupan *Phil.*	120E2
Dakar *Sen.*	140B5
Da Lat *Viet.*	119C2
Dali *China*	117E4
Dallas *USA*	23D2
Dalmally *Scot*	62D4
Daloa *Côte d'Ivoire*	144B2
Da Nang *Viet.*	119C2
Dandong *China*	112G2
Dar'ā *Syria*	130B2
Dar el Beida *Mor.*	140C3
Dar es Salaam *Tanz.*	147G5
Darlington *Eng*	55F3
Darmstadt *FRG*	90B3
Daroca *Spain*	74B1
Daru *PNG*	125G4
Darwin *Aust.*	154C2
Datong *China*	112F2
Daugavpils *Latvia*	102D4
Dauphine Province *France*	71D3
Davao *Phil.*	120E3
David *Panama*	25C5
Dawson Creek *Canada*	13F4
Dax *France*	69B3
Dayton *USA*	18E2
Daytona Beach *USA*	20E3
D'Entrecasteaux I. *PNG*	125H4
De Aar *S.Africa*	149C4
Debre Mark'os *Eth.*	147G3
Debrecen *Hung.*	88E3
Dehra Dun *India*	126F2
Delaware State *USA*	19F2
Delhi *India*	126F3
Den Helder *Neth.*	84A2
Denbigh *Wales*	53D4
Denizli *Turk.*	130A2
Denver *USA*	17C2
Derby *Eng*	55F5
Des Moines *USA*	18D1
Desé *Eth.*	147G3
Dessau *FRG*	85C2
Detroit *USA*	18E1
Deva *Rom.*	88E3
Devon I. *Canada*	14K2
Dezfūl *Iran*	131C2
Dezhou *China*	112F3
Dhāka *Bang.*	127H3
Ídhra *Greece*	81E3
Dibrugarh *India*	127H3

178

Place	Ref.
Didcot *Eng*	56F6
Dieppe *France*	68C2
Dijon *France*	70C2
Dili *Indon.*	124E4
Dimashq *Syria*	130B2
Dimitrovgrad *Bulg.*	83F2
Dingle *Ireland*	66A4
Dingwall *Scot*	60D3
Diré Dawa *Eth.*	147H4
Ādīs Ābeba *Eth.*	147G4
Disko I. *Greenland*	14N3
Dist. Fed. State *Brazil*	37E4
Diyarbakir *Turk.*	130B2
Djelfa *Alg.*	141D3
Djibouti *Djibouti*	147H3
Dnepropetrovsk *Ukraine*	108E5
Dobreta-Turnu-Severin *Rom.*	.82E2
Dodoma *Tanz.*	147G5
Dôle *France*	70D2
Dolgellau *Wales*	58D5
Dombås *Nor.*	92B3
Dominica I. *Caribbean*	27G3
Domodossola *Italy*	76B1
Doncaster *Eng*	55F4
Donegal *Ireland*	64C2
Donetsk *Russia*	108E5
Dorchester *Eng*	59E7
Dornie *Scot*	60C3
Dortmund *FRG*	84B2
Douala *Cameroon*	145D2
Douglas *Isle of Man*	53C3
Dourados *Brazil*	38E5
Dover *Eng*	56J6
Dover *USA*	19F2
Dráma *Greece*	81E2
Drammen *Nor.*	94C4
Dresden *FRG*	91C2
Drogheda *Ireland*	67E3
Dubayy *UAE*	133D3
Dublin *Ireland*	67E3
Dubrovnik *Cro.*	82D2
Ducie I. *Pacific O.*	162
Dudley *Eng*	58E5
Dugi I. *Cro.*	77C2
Duisburg *FRG*	84B2
Dukou *China*	117E4
Duluth *USA*	18D1
Dumbarton *Scot*	62D5
Dumfries *Scot*	63E5
Dun Laoghaire *Ireland*	67E3
Dunbar *Scot*	63F5
Dundalk *Ireland*	65E2
Dundee *Scot*	63F4
Dundrum *N.Ire.*	65F2
Dunedin *NZ*	157G5
Dunfermline *Scot*	63E4
Dungarvan *Ireland*	67D4
Dungiven *N.Ire.*	65E2
Dunkeld *Scot*	62E4
Dunkerque *France*	68C1
Dunleer *Ireland*	65E3
Durban *S.Africa*	151D3
Durham *Eng*	54F3
Durham *USA*	18F2
Durness *Scot*	60D2
Durrës *Alb.*	80D2
Durrow *Ireland*	67D4
Dushanbe *Tajikistan*	109H6
Dusseldorf *FRG*	84B2
Duyun *China*	117E4

E

Place	Ref.
Eastbourne *Eng*	57H7
East Falkland I. *South Atlantic O.*	39D3
East Kilbride *Scot*	63D5
East London *S.Africa*	149C4
Eboli *Italy*	79D2
Ecija *Spain*	73A2
Eday I. *Scot*	61F1
Edgeworthstown *Ireland*	67D3
Edinburgh *Scot*	63E5
Edmonton *Canada*	13G4
Efate I. *Vanuatu*	156F2
Egadi I. *Italy*	78C3
Egersund *Nor.*	94B4
Eigg I. *Scot*	62B4
Eindhoven *Neth.*	84B2
Eisenach *FRG*	91C2
Elba I. *Italy*	76C2
Elblag *Pol.*	86D2
Elche *Spain*	75B2
El Djouf *Maur*	140C4
El Dorado *Ven.*	34C2
Eldoret *Kenya*	147G4
Eleuthera I. *The Bahamas*	24D1
El Faiyûm *Egypt*	142G2
El Fasher *Sudan*	146F3
El Ferrol *Spain*	72A1
El Gîza *Egypt*	142G1
El Golea *Alg.*	141D3
El Iskandarîya *Egypt*	142F1
El Khartum *Sudan*	142G3
Ellesmere I. *Canada*	14K2
Ellesmere Port *Eng*	53E4
Ellon *Scot*	61F3
El Minya *Egypt*	142G2
El Obeid *Sudan*	146G3
El Paso *USA*	23C2
El Qâhira *Egypt*	142G1
Elvas *Port.*	73A2
Ely *Eng*	56H5
Enarración *Par.*	38E5
Ende *Indon.*	124E4
Enggano I. *Indon.*	122C4
Enna *Italy*	79C3
Ennis *Ireland*	66B4
Enniscorthy *Ireland*	67E4
Enniskillen *N.Ire.*	65D2
Ennistymon *Ireland*	66B4
Enschede *Neth.*	84B2
Entebbe *Uganda*	146G4
Enugu *Nig.*	145D2
Epi I. *Vanuatu*	156F2
Erenhot *China*	112F2
Erfurt *FRG*	91C2
Eriskay I. *Scot*	60A3
Erlangen *FRG*	91C3
Erromanga I. *Vanuatu*	156F2
Erzurum *Turk.*	130C2
Esbjerg *Den.*	94B4
Esfahân *Iran*	131D2
Eskisehir *Turk.*	130B2
Esperance *Aust.*	155B4
Espírito Santo *Brazil*	37E4
Espíritu Santo I. *Vanuatu*	156F2
Espoo *Fin*	95E3
Essaouira *Mor.*	140C3
Essen *FRG*	84B2
Estremoz *Port.*	73A2
Evansville *USA*	18E2
Evvoia I. *Greece*	81E3
Exeter *Eng*	59D7
Extremadura Region *Spain*	73A2

F

Place	Ref.
Faeroes I. *Den.*	92A2
Fair I. *Scot*	61J8
Fairbanks *USA*	12D3
Faisalâbâd *Pak.*	126F4
Fakfak *Indon.*	124F4
Falcarragh *Ireland*	64C1
Falkirk *Scot*	63E4
Falkland Islands *South Atlantic O.*	39D8
Falmouth *Eng*	59B7
Falster I. *Den.*	94C5
Falun *Sweden*	94D3
Fano *Italy*	77C2
Farâh *Afghan.*	131E2
Fareham *Eng*	57F7
Fargo *USA*	17D1
Faro *Port.*	73A2
Faroe I. *Den.*	92A2
Farquhar Is. *Indian O.*	150F1
Fauske *Nor.*	92D2
Faya-Largeau *Chad*	142E3
Fdérik *Maur.*	140B4
Felixstowe *Eng*	56J6
Fergana *Uzbekistan*	109J5
Ferkessédougou *Côte d'Ivoire*	144B2
Fermoy *Ireland*	66C4
Ferrara *Italy*	77C2
Fés *Mor.*	140C3
Fetlar I. *Scot*	61K7
Feyzâbâd *Afghan.*	126F2
Fianarantsoa *Madag.*	151E3
Figueras *Spain*	74C1
Fiji Is. *Pacific O.*	165
Filiasi *Rom.*	82E2
Firenze *Italy*	77C2
Fishguard *Wales*	58C6
Fitzroy Crossing *Aust.*	154B2
Fleetwood *Eng*	53D4
Flensburg *FRG*	84B2
Flores I. *Kiribati*	162
Flores I. *Indon.*	124E4
Flores *Guatemala*	24B3
Florianópolis *Brazil*	38F5
Florida State *USA*	20E3
Focsani *Rom*	89F3
Foggia *Italy*	79D2
Foligno *Italy*	77C2
Follonica *Italy*	76C2
Forfar *Scot*	63F4
Forli *Italy*	77C2
Formentera *Spain*	75C2
Formia *Italy*	79C2
Formosa State *Arg.*	40C5
Fortaleza *Brazil*	37F3
Fort Augustus *Scot*	60D3
Fort-de-France *Martinique*	27G4
Fort Lauderdale *USA*	21E3
Fort Simpson *Canada*	12F3

Fort William *Scot*	62C4
Fort Yukon *USA*	12D3
Fort Worth *USA*	23D2
Foshan *China*	114F4
Foula *I. Scot*	61H7
Fougéres *France*	68B2
Foz do Iguacu *Brazil*	38E5
Fraga *Spain*	74C1
Franca *Brazil*	37E5
Franceville *Gabon*	145E3
Franche-Comte Province *France*	71D2
Francistown *Botswana*	149C3
Frankfort *USA*	18E2
Frankfurt *FRG*	90B2
Fraser *I. Aust.*	156E3
Fraserburgh *Scot*	61F3
Frederikshåb *Greenland*	14O3
Frederikshavn *Den.*	94C4
Frederikstad *Nor.*	94C4
Freetown *Sierra Leone*	144A2
Freiburg *FRG*	90B3
Fremantle *Aust.*	155A4
Fresno *USA*	16B2
Frosinone *Italy*	77C2
Ft. Wayne *USA*	18E1
Fuerteventura *I. Canary Is.*	140B4
Fujian Province *China*	114F4
Fukui *Japan*	115M8
Fukuoka *Japan*	115H3
Fukushima *Japan*	115P8
Funchal *Madeira*	140B3
Furneaux Group *I. Aust.*	157D5
Fürth *FRG.*	91C3
Furukawa *Japan*	115P7
Fushun *China*	112G2
Fuxin *China*	112G2
Fuzhou *China*	114F4
Fyn *I. Den.*	94C4

G

Gabès *Tunisia*	141D3
Gaborone *Botswana*	149C3
Gainsborough *Eng*	55G4
Gairloch *Scot*	60C3
Galashiels *Scot*	63F5
Galati *Rom.*	89F3
Galicia Region *Spain*	72A1
Galle *Sri Lanka*	129G5
Gallipoli *Italy*	79D2
Gällivare *Sweden*	93E2
Galveston *USA*	20D3
Galway *Ireland*	66B3
Gambier Is. *Pacific O.*	162
Gambona *Congo*	145E3
Gandia *Spain*	75B2
Ganzhou *China*	114F4
Gao *Mali*	141C3
Garve *Scot*	60D3
Gascogne Province *France*	69B3
Gateshead *Eng*	54F3
Gauhati *India*	127H3
Gävle *Sweden*	94D3
Gaziantep *Turk.*	130B2
Gdansk *Pol.*	86D2
Gdynia *Pol.*	86D2
Gedaref *Sudan*	147G3
Geelong *Aust.*	157D4
Gejiu *China*	117E4

Gela *Italy*	79C3
Gelati *Rom.*	89F3
General Santos *Phil.*	120E3
Genéve *Switz.*	71D2
Genova *Italy*	76B2
Gent *Belg.*	70C1
George Town *Malay.*	122C3
Georgetown *Guyana*	34D2
Georgetown *St. Vincent*	27G4
Georgia State *USA*	20E2
Gera *FRG*	91C2
Geraldton *Aust.*	155A3
Gerona *Spain*	74C1
Getafe *Spain*	72B1
Gevgelija *Yugos.*	80E2
Ghàdàmis *Libya*	141D3
Ghât *Libya*	141E4
Gibraltar Colony *SW Europe*	73A2
Gifu *Japan*	115M9
Giglio *I. Italy*	76C2
Gijón *Spain*	72A1
Gilbert Is. *Kiribati*	165
Gilgit *Pak.*	126F2
Girvan *Scot*	62D5
Gisborne *NZ*	157G4
Giurgiu *Rom.*	83F2
Glasgow *Scot*	63D5
Glenrothes *Scot*	63E4
Gliwice *Pol.*	88D2
Gloucester *Eng*	58E6
Gniezno *Pol.*	85D2
Gobabis *Namibia*	149B3
Godthåb *Greenland*	14N3
Goiânia *Brazil*	37E4
Goiás State *Brazil*	37E4
Gol *Nor.*	94B3
Golmund *China*	111D3
Gomel' *Belarus*	102E4
Gomera *Canary Is.*	140B4
Gonaïves *Haiti*	26E3
Gonder *Eth.*	147G3
Goole *Eng*	55G4
Gorontalo *Indon.*	124E3
Gort *Ireland*	66C3
Gorzów Wielkopolski *Pol.*	85D2
Göteborg *Sweden*	94C4
Gotland *I. Sweden*	95D4
Gottingen *FRG*	84B2
Goulburn *Aust.*	157D4
Gran Canaria *Canary Is.*	140B4
Granada *Nic.*	25B4
Granada *Spain*	73B2
Grand Bahama I. *The Bahamas*	24D1
Grand Rapids *USA*	18E1
Grandola *Port.*	73A2
Graz *Aust.*	91D3
Great Abaco I. *The Bahamas*	24D1
Great Exuma I. *The Bahamas*	24D2
Great Inagua I. *The Bahamas*	26E2
Great Nicobar I. *India*	129H5
Great Yarmouth *Eng*	56J5
Greater Antilles Is. *Car*	24D3
Greenland Dependency *N.A.*	14O2
Greenock *Scot*	62D5

Greensboro *USA*	18F2
Grenada *Caribbean Sea*	27G4
Grenada, *I. Caribbean*	27G4
Grenadines Is., *The. Caribbean*	27G4
Gretna *Scot*	63E5
Grimsby *Eng*	55G4
Grong *Nor.*	92C3
Groningen *Neth.*	84B2
Groote Eylandt *I. Aust.*	154C2
Grootfontein *Namibia*	149B2
Grosseto *Italy*	77C2
Groznyy *Russia*	108F5
Grudziadz *Pol.*	86D2
Guadalajara *Mexico*	23C3
Guadalajara *Spain*	72B1
Guadalcanal I. *Solomon Is.*	156E2
Guadalupe I. *Mexico*	22B3
Guadeloupe *I. Caribbean Sea*	26G3
Guam *Pacific O.*	121G2
Guangdong Province *China*	117E4
Guangxi Province *China*	117E4
Guangzhou *China*	114F4
Guantánamo *Cuba*	26D2
Guarda *Port.*	72A1
Guatemala *Guatemala*	25A4
Guayaquil *Ecuador*	35B3
Guernsey *I. UK*	59E8
Guildford *Eng*	56G6
Guilin *China*	114F4
Guiria *Ven.*	34C1
Guiyang *China*	117E4
Guizhou Province *China*	117E4
Gulu *Uganda*	146G4
Guyenne Province *France*	69B3
Gwalior *India*	126F3
Gweru *Zim.*	149C2
Gyor *Hung.*	88D3

H

Hå'il *S.Arabia*	130C3
Haarlem *Neth.*	84A2
Hachinohe *Japan*	115P6
Hagen *FRG*	84B2
Haifa *Israel*	130B2
Haikou *China*	114F4
Hailar *China*	112F2
Hainan Dao *I. China*	114F5
Haiphong *Viet.*	119C1
Hakodate *Japan*	113J2
Halab *Syria*	130B2
Halden *Nor.*	94C4
Halifax *Canada*	15M5
Halifax *Eng*	55F4
Halle *FRG*	85C2
Halmahera *I. Indon.*	124E3
Halmstad *Sweden*	94C4
Hamadån *Iran*	131C2
Hamamatsu *Japan*	115M9
Hamar *Nor.*	94C3
Hamburg *FRG*	85C2
Hamhung *N.Korea*	112G2
Hami *China*	111D2
Hamilton *Canada*	15K5
Hamilton *NZ*	157G4
Hamm *FRG*	84B2
Hammerfest *Nor.*	93E1

Hanamaki *Japan*	115P7
Handan *China*	112F3
Hangzhou *China*	114G3
Hannover *FRG*	84B2
Hanoi *Viet.*	119C1
Hanzhong *China*	117E3
Hāora *India*	129G3
Harare *Zim.*	150D2
Harbin *China*	112G2
Hårer *Eth.*	147H4
Hargeysa *Somalia*	147H4
Harlow *Eng*	56H6
Harris I. *Scot*	60B3
Harrisburg *USA*	18F1
Harrogate *Eng*	55F4
Hartford *USA*	19F1
Hartlepool *Eng*	54F3
Harwich *Eng*	56J6
Hässleholm *Sweden*	94C4
Hastings *Eng*	57H7
Hastings *NZ*	157G4
Haugesund *Nor.*	94B4
Havana (La Habana)*Cuba*	24C2
Havant *Eng*	57G7
Hawaii *Hawaiian Is.*	22H
Hawaiian Is. *Pacific O.*	22H
Hawick *Scot*	63F5
Hay River *Canada*	13G3
Heanor *Eng*	55F4
Heard Is. *Indian O.*	164
Hebei *China*	112F3
Hefei *China*	114F3
Hegang *China*	112H2
Heidelberg *FRG*	90B3
Heilongjiang Province *China*	112G2
Helena *USA*	17B1
Hella *Iceland*	92A2
Hellín *Spain*	75B2
Helmsdale *Scot*	61E2
Helsingborg *Sweden*	94C4
Helsingfors *Fin*	95F3
Helsinki *Fin*	95F3
Henan Province *China*	114F3
Hengyang *China*	114F4
Henzada *Myanmar*	118B2
Herāt *Afghan.*	131E2
Hereford *Eng*	58E5
Hermosillo *USA*	23B3
Hexham *Eng*	52E3
Hierro *Canary Is.*	140B4
Hiiumaa I. *Estonia*	95E4
Himeji *Japan*	115L9
Hims *Syria*	130B2
Hinckley *Eng*	56F5
Hinnøy I. *Nor.*	92D2
Hiroshima *Japan*	113H3
Hîrsova *Rom.*	83F2
Hispaniola I. *Caribbean Sea*	26E3
Hitachi *Japan*	115P8
Ho Chi Minh City *Viet.*	119C2
Hobart *Tasmania*	157D5
Höfn *Iceland*	92B2
Hohhot *China*	112F2
Hokitika *NZ*	157G5
Hokkaidō I. *Japan*	113J2
Holguín *Cuba*	24D2
Holy I. *Eng*	54F2

Holyhead *Wales*	53C4
Honiara *Solomon Is.*	156E1
Honolulu *Hawaiian Is.*	22H
Horsham *Eng*	56G6
Hotan *China*	110C3
Hotan *China*	126F2
Hoting *Sweden*	92D3
Houghton-le-Spring *Eng*	54F3
Houston *USA*	20D3
Hovd *Mongolia*	111D2
Hoy I. *Scot*	61E2
Hradec-Králové *Czech.*	91D2
Huainan *China*	114F3
Huambo *Angola*	148B2
Huancayo *Peru*	35B4
Huangshi *China*	114F3
Hubei Province *China*	114F3
Hubli *India*	128F4
Huddersfield *Eng*	55F4
Hudiksvall *Sweden*	94D3
Hue *Viet.*	119C2
Huelva *Spain*	73A2
Hughenden *Aust.*	156D3
Humaitá *Brazil*	35C3
Hunan Province *China*	114F4
Hunstanton *Eng*	55H5
Huntly *Scot*	61F3
Huntsville *USA*	18E2
Húsavik *Iceland*	92B1
Hvar I. *Cro.*	77D2
Hwange *China*	148C2
Hyderābād *India*	128F4
Hyderābād *Pak.*	126E3
Hythe *Eng*	56J6l

I	
Ibadan *Nig.*	145D2
Ibiza *Spain*	75C2
Ibiza I. *Spain*	75C2
Ica *Peru*	35B4
Iceland Republic *N.Atlantic O.*	14R3
Idaho State *USA*	16B1
Igarka *Russia*	103K3
Igoumenitsa *Greece*	80E3
Ikaría I. *Greece*	81F3
Ile d'Oléron *France*	69B2
Ile de Noirmoutier *France*	68B2
Ile de Ré *France*	69B2
Ilebo *Dem.Rep.of Congo*	146F5
Iles d'Hyères *France*	71D3
Ilfracombe *Eng*	58C6
Iliodhrómia I. *Greece*	81E3
Illinois State *USA*	18E1
Iloilo *Phil.*	120E2
Ilorin *Nig.*	145D2
Imperatriz *Brazil*	37E3
Impfondo *Congo*	146E4
Imphāl *India*	127H3
In Salah *Alg.*	141D4
Indiana State *USA*	18E2
Indianapolis *USA*	18E2
Indore *India*	128F3
Inhambane *Mozam.*	151D3
Inner Hebrides *Scot*	62B3
Inner Mongolia Province *China*	112F2
Innsbruck *Aust.*	91C3
Inuvik *Canada*	12E3

Inveraray *Scot*	62C4
Invercargill *NZ*	157F5
Inverness *Scot*	61D3
Inverurie *Scot*	61F3
Ioannina *Greece*	80E3
Ios I. *Greece*	81F3
Iowa State *USA*	18D1
Ipoh *Malay.*	122C3
Iquique *Chile*	35B5
Iquitos *Peru*	35B3
Iráklion *Greece*	81F3
Iringa *Tanz.*	150D1
Irkutsk *Russia*	106M4
Irvine *Scot*	62D5
Isafördhur *Iceland*	92A1
Ischia I. *Italy*	79C2
Ise *Japan*	115M9
Ishinomaki *Japan*	115P7
Isiro *Dem. Rep. of Congo*	146F4
Isla Blanquilla I. *Ven.*	27G4
Isla Coiba *Panama*	25C5
Isla de Chilloé I. *Chile*	41B7
Isla de la Bahia *Hondur.*	24B3
Isla de la Juventud *Cuba*	24C2
Isla del Rey *Panama*	25D5
Isla Los Rogues I. *Ven.*	27F4
Isla Margarita I. *Ven.*	27G4
Isla Santa Inés I. *Chile*	41B7
Islāmābād *Pak.*	126F2
Island of Newfoundland *Canada*	15N4
Islas Canarias *Spain*	140B4
Islay I. *Scot*	62B5
Isle of Man *UK*	53C3
Isle of Wight *Eng*	57F7
Isles of Scilly *Eng*	59A8
Istanbul *Turk.*	130A1
Isthmus of Kra *Thai*	118B3
Itabuna *Brazil*	37F4
Itaituba *Brazil*	37D3
Iturup I. *Russia*	113J2
Ivalo *Fin*	93F2
Ivangrad *Yugos.*	82D2
Ivanovo *Russia*	102F4
Iwaki *Japan*	115P8
Iwo Jima *Japan*	121G1
Izhevsk *Russia*	109G4
Izmir *Turk.*	130A2

J	
Jabalpur *India*	128F3
Jackson *USA*	20D2
Jacksonville *USA*	20E2
Jacmel *Haiti*	26E3
Jaén *Spain*	73B2
Jaffna *Sri Lanka*	129G5
Jaipur *India*	126F3
Jajce *Bos.Herz.*	77D2
Jakarta *Indon.*	123C4
Jalgaon *India*	128F3
Jamaica *Caribbean*	122C4
Jambi *Indon.*	126F2
Jammu *India*	126F2
Jamnager *India*	128E3
Jämsänkoski *Fin*	95F3
Jamshedpur *India*	129G3
Jardines de la Reina *Cuba*	24D2
Jarvis I. *Pacific O*	162
Jawa I. *Indon.*	123C4

Jayapura *Indon.*	125G4
Jedburgh *Scot*	63F5
Jefferson City *USA*	18D2
Jelenia Góra *Pol.*	91D2
Jena *FRG*	91C2
Jequié *Brazil*	37E4
Jerez de la Frontera *Spain*	73A2
Jersey I. *UK*	59E8
Jerusalem *Israel*	130B2
Jhansi *India*	126F3
Ji'an *China*	114F4
Jiamusi *China*	112H2
Jiangsu Province *China*	114F3
Jiangxi Province *China*	114F4
Jiddah *S.Arabia*	132B3
Jihlava *Czech.*	91D3
Jilin *China*	112G2
Jilin Province *China*	113G2
Jima *Eth.*	147G4
Jinan *China*	112F3
Jingdezhen *China*	114F4
Jinhua *China*	114F4
Jining *China*	114F3
Jinja *Uganda*	146G4
Jinzhou *China*	112G2
Jiujiang *China*	114F4
João Pessoa *Brazil*	37F3
Jodhpur *India*	126F3
Johannesburg *S.Africa*	149C3
John O'Groats *Scot*	61E2
Johnson I. *Pacific O.*	159
Johor Baharu *Malay.*	122C3
Jokkmokk *Sweden*	93D2
Jólo I. *Phil.*	120E3
Jönköping *Sweden*	94C4
Jörn *Sweden*	93E2
Jos *Nig.*	145D2
Jotunheimen *Nor.*	94B3
Juázeiro *Brazil*	37E3
Juba *Sudan*	146G4
Jujuy State *Arg.*	40C5
Julianehåb *Greenland*	14O3
Juneau *USA*	12E4
Jura I. *Scot*	62C5
Jylland I. *Den.*	94B4
Jyväskylä *Fin*	93F3

K

Kábul *Afghan.*	126E2
Kaduna *Nig.*	145D1
Kaédi *Maur.*	140B5
Kaesŏng *N.Korea*	112G3
Kagoshima *Japan*	115H3
Kaifeng *China*	114F3
Kailua *Hawaiian Is.*	22H
Kairouan *Tunisia*	141D3
Kajaani *Fin*	93F3
Kākināda *India*	129G4
Kalabáka *Greece*	80E3
Kalajoki *Fin*	93E3
Kalámai *Greece*	80E3
Kalaupapa *Hawaiian Is.*	22H
Kalémié	
Dem. Rep. of Congo	146F5
Kalgoorlie *Aust.*	155B4
Kálimnos I. *Greece*	81F3
Kaliningrad *Russia*	102D4
Kalisz *Pol.*	86D2
Kalmar *Sweden*	94D4

Kamaishi *Japan*	115P7
Kamina	
Dam. Rep. of Congo	148C1
Kamloops *Canada*	13F4
Kampala *Uganda*	146G4
Kananga	
Dem. Rep. of Congo	146F5
Kanazawa *Japan*	115M8
Kandahár *Afghan.*	126E2
Kandalaksha *Russia*	102E3
Kandangan *Indon.*	123D4
Kandy *Sri Lanka*	129G5
Kaneohe *Hawaiian Is*	22H
Kangaroo I. *Aust.*	155C4
Kano *Nig.*	145D1
Kansas City *USA*	18D2
Kansas State *USA*	17D2
Kao-hsiung *Taiwan*	120E1
Kaolack *Sen.*	144A1
Karáchi *Pak.*	128E3
Karaganda *Kazakhstan*	109J5
Karbalá *Iraq*	130B2
Karcag *Hung.*	88E3
Karlobag *Cro.*	77D2
Karlovac *Cro.*	77D1
Karlshamn *Sweden*	94C4
Karlskoga *Sweden*	94C4
Karlskrona *Sweden*	94D4
Karlsruhe *FRG*	90B3
Karlstad *Sweden*	94C4
Kárpathos I. *Greece*	81F3
Karshi *Uzbekistan*	109H6
Kasama *Zim.*	150D2
Kasese *Uganda*	146G4
Kashi *China*	110B3
Kásos I. *Greece*	81F3
Kassala *Sudan*	143G3
Kassel *FRG*	90B2
Kastoria *Greece*	80E2
Kateríni *Greece*	80E2
Katherine *Aust.*	154C2
Kathmandu *Nepal*	127G3
Katowice *Pol.*	88D2
Katsina *Nig.*	145D1
Kauai I. *Hawaiian Is.*	22H
Kaunas *Lithuania*	95E5
Kaválla *Greece*	81E2
Kawaihae *Hawaiian Is.*	22H
Kawasaki *Japan*	115N9
Kayes *Mali*	144A1
Kayseri *Turk.*	130B2
Kazan *Russia*	108F4
Kazanlŭk *Bulg.*	83F2
Kazan-rettó *Japan*	121G1
Kéa *Greece*	81E3
Kecskemét *Hung.*	88D3
Kediri *Indon.*	123D4
Keetmanshoop *Namibia*	149B3
Kefallinía I. *Greece*	80E3
Keflavik *Iceland*	92A2
Keighley *Eng*	55F4
Keith *Scot*	61F3
Kelang *Malay.*	122C3
Kells *Ireland*	67E3
Kemerovo *Russia*	109K4
Kemi *Fin*	93E2
Kemijarvi *Fin*	93F2

Kendal *Eng*	53E3
Kendari *Indon.*	124E4
Kengtung *Myanmar*	118B1
Kenitra *Mor.*	140C3
Kenmare *Ireland*	66B5
Kenora *Canada*	15J5
Kentucky State *USA*	18E2
Kep.Anambas I. *Indon*	123C3
Kep.Aru I. *Indon.*	124F4
Kep. Banggai *Indon.*	124E4
Kep. Kai I. *Indon.*	124F4
Kep. Leti I. *Indon.*	124E4
Kep. Mentawai, Arch.	
Indon.	122B4
Kepno *Pol.*	88D2
Kep. Sangihe I. *Indon*	124E3
Kep. Sula *Indon.*	124E4
Kep. Talaud I. *Indon.*	124E3
Kep. Tanimbar I.	124F4
Kep. Togian *Indon.*	124E4
Kerch *Russia*	108E5
Kerguelen Is. *Indian O.*	164
Kérkira *Greece*	80D3
Kermadec Is. *Pacific O.*	165
Kermán *Iran*	131D2
Keswick *Eng*	52E3
Key West *USA*	20E3
Khabarovsk *Russia*	107P5
Khalkis *Greece*	81E3
Khaniá *Greece*	81E3
Khar'kov *Russia*	108E4
Kharagpur *India*	129G3
Khartoum North *Sudan*	142G3
Khartoum *Sudan*	142G3
Khíos I. *Greece*	81F3
Khulna *Bang.*	129G3
Kiel *FRG*	85C2
Kielce *Pol.*	88E2
Kigali *Rwanda*	146G5
Kigoma *Tanz.*	146F5
Kikladhes Is. *Greece*	81E3
Kikwit *Dem. Rep. of Congo*	146E5
Kildare *Ireland*	67E3
Kilkenny *Ireland*	67D4
Killarney *Ireland*	66B4
Kilmarnock *Scot*	62D5
Kilrush *Ireland*	66B4
Kimberley *S.Africa*	149C3
Kindia *Guinea*	144A1
Kindu *Dem. Rep. of Congo*	146F5
King I. *Aust.*	157D4
Kings Lynn *Eng*	55H5
Kingston *Jamaica*	24D3
Kingston-upon-Hull *Eng*	55G4
Kingswood *Eng*	58E6
Kingussie *Scot*	61D3
Kinnegad *Ireland*	67D3
Kintyre *Scot*	62C5
Kinvarra *Ireland*	66C3
Kiribati Is. *Pacific O.*	165
Kiritimati *Kiribati*	162
Kirkby Stephen *Eng*	53E3
Kirkcaldy *Scot*	63E4
Kirkenes *Nor.*	93G2
Kirkūk *Iraq*	130C2
Kirkwall *Scot*	61F2
Kirov *Russia*	108F4
Kirovabad *Ukraine*	108F5
Kiruna *Sweden*	93E2

Kisangani
  Dem. Rep. of Congo 146F4
Kiskunfélegyháza *Hung* 88D3
Kismaayo *Somalia* 147H5
Kisumu *Kenya* 147G5
Kita-Kyūshū *Japan* 113H3
Kíthira I. *Greece* 81E3
Kíthnos *Greece* 81E3
Kitwe *Zambia* 148C2
Kiyev *Ukraine* 102E4
Kladno *Czech.Rep.* 91C2
Klagenfurt *Aust.* 91C3
Klaipeda *Lithuania* 102D4
Klerksdorp *S.Africa* 149C3
Knoxville *USA* 18E2
Kōbe *Japan* 115L9
København *Den.* 94C4
Koblenz *FRG* 90B2
Kochi *Japan* 113H3
Kodiak I. 22J
Kofu *Japan* 115N9
Kokkola *Fin* 93E3
Kolding *Den.* 94B4
Kolhapur *India* 128F4
Köln *FRG* 90B2
Koloma *Russia* 102E4
Kolwezi
  Dem. Rep. of Congo 148C2
Komatsu *Japan* 115M8
Komotiní *Greece* 81F2
Kompong Cham *Camb.* 119C2
Kompong Som *Camb.* 118C2
Komsomol'sk na-Amure
  Russia 107P4
Konin *Pol.* 86D2
Konjic *Bos. Herz.* 82D2
Konya *Turk.* 130B2
Kópavogur *Iceland* 92A2
Korçë *Alb.* 80E2
Korcula I. *Cro.* 77D2
Kórinthos *Greece* 80E3
Koriyama *Japan* 115P8
Kornat I. *Cro.* 77D2
Korsör *Den.* 94C4
Kós I. *Greece* 81F3
Kosice *Slovakia* 88E3
Kosovska-Mitrovica *Yugos.* 82E2
Koszalin *Pol* 85D2
Kota *India* 126F3
Kota Baharu *Malay.* 122C3
Kota Kinabalu *Malay.* 123D3
Kotka *Fin* 95F3
Kotlas *Russia* 102F3
Kotor *Yugos.* 82D2
Kowloon *Hong Kong* 119D1
Kragujevac *Yugos.* 82E2
Kraków *Pol.* 88D2
Kramsfors *Sweden* 92D3
Kranj *Slovenia* 77C1
Krasnodar *Russia* 108E5
Krasnovodsk *Turkmenistan* 108G5
Krasnoyarsk *Russia* 106L4
Krefeld *FRG* 84B2
Kristiansand *Nor.* 94B4
Kristianstad *Sweden* 94C4
Krivoy Rog *Ukraine* 108E5
Krk I. *Cro.* 77C1
Kruscevac *Yugos.* 82E2
Kuala Lumpur *Malay.* 122C3

Kuala Terengganu *Malay.* 122C3
Kuching *Malay.* 123D3
Kulata *Bulg.* 82E2
Kumamoto *Japan* 115H3
Kumanovo *Macedonia.* 82E2
Kumasi *Ghana* 144B2
Kunashir I. *Russia* 113J2
Kunming *China* 117E4
Kuopio *Fin* 93F3
Kupang *Indon.* 124E5
Kuril'skye Ostrova *Russia* 107R5
Kurnool *India* 128F4
Kursk *Russia* 108E4
Kushiro *Japan* 113J2
Kwangju *S.Korea* 112G3
Kyle of Lochalsh *Scot* 60C3
Kyoto *Japan* 115L9
Kyzyl *Russia* 106L4
Kzyl Orda *Kazakhstan.* 109H5

L

Laâyoune *Mor.* 140B4
Labé *Guinea* 144A1
Lábrea *Brazil* 35C3
Labytnangi *Russia* 103H3
La Ceiba *Honduras* 25B4
La Coruña *Spain* 72A1
Lae *PNG* 125G4
La Fléche *France* 68B2
Lagos *Nig.* 145D2
Lagos *Port.* 73A2
La Habana (Havana) *Cuba* 24C2
Lahore *Pak.* 126F2
Lahti *Fin* 95F3
Lai Chau *Viet.* 118C1
Lairg *Scot* 60D2
Lajes *Brazil* 128F4
Lakshadweep Is. *India* 128F4
Lambaréné *Gabon* 145E3
Lamía *Greece* 80E3
Lampedusa I. *Italy* 79C3
Lampione I. *Italy* 78C3
Lanai I. *Hawaiian Is.* 22H
Lanark *Scot* 63E5
Lancaster *Eng* 53E3
Lang Son *Viet.* 70D2
Langres *France* 71C3
Languedoc Province *Fran* 71C3
Lansing *USA* 18E1
Lanzarote I. *Canary Is.* 140B4
Lanzhou *China* 113E3
Laoag *Phil.* 120E2
Lao Cai *Viet.* 119C1
La Palma I. *Canary Is.* 140B4
La Pampa State *Arg.* 40C6
La Paz *Bolivia* 35C4
La Plata *Arg.* 38E6
Laredo *USA* 23D3
Largs *Scot* 62D2
La Rioja Region *Spain* 72B1
La Rioja State *Arg.* 40C5
Lárisa *Greece* 80E3
Larne *N.Ire.* 65F2
La Rochelle *France* 69B2
La Roda *Spain* 75B2
La Romana *Dom. Republic* 26F3
La Serena *Chile* 40B5
Lashio *Myanmar* 118B1
Iasi *Rom.* 89F3

Las Palmas de Gran Canaria
  Canary is. 140B4
La Spezia *Italy* 76B2
Lastovo I. *Cro.* 77D2
Las Vegas *USA* 16B2
Latina *Italy* 79C2
La Tortuga I. *Ven.* 27F4
Launceston *Tasmania* 157D5
Laurenceikirk *Scot* 63F4
Lausanne *Switz.* 71D2
Laut I. *Indon.* 123D4
Laval *France* 68B2
L'Aquila *Italy* 77C2
Leeds *Eng* 55F4
Leeuwarden *Neth.* 84B2
Leeward Is. *Caribbean Sea* 26G3
Legazpi *Phil.* 120E2
Leicester *Eng* 56F5
Leipzig *FRG* 91C2
Leiria *Port.* 72A2
Le Havre *France* 68C2
Le Mans *France* 68C2
Lens *France* 70C1
León *Mexico* 23C3
León *Nic.* 25B4
León *Spain* 72A1
Lérida *Spain* 74C1
Léros I. *Greece* 81F3
Lerwick *Scot* 61J7
Les Caye *Haiti* 26E3
Leshan *China* 117E4
Leskovac *Yugos.* 82E2
Lesotho, Kingdom *S.Africa* 149C3
Lesser Antilles Is. *Carib.* 27F4
Lésvós I. *Greece* 81F3
Letterkenny *Ireland* 65D2
Levkás I. *Greece* 80E3
Lewes *Eng* 57H7
Lewis I. *Scot* 60B2
Leyte I. *Phil.* 120E2
Lhasa *China* 116D4
Lianoyang *China* 112G2
Lianyungang *China* 114F3
Liaoning Province *China* 112G3
Liaoyuan *China* 112G2
Liberec *Czech.Rep.* 91D2
Libreville *Gabon* 145D2
Lichinga *Mozam.* 150D2
Liège *Belg.* 70D1
Liepāja *Latvia* 95E4
Likasi *Dem. Rep. of Congo* 148C2
Lille *France* 70C1
Lillehammer *Nor.* 94C3
Lilongwe *Malawi* 150D2
Lima *Peru* 35B4
Limerick *Ireland* 66C4
Límnos *Greece* 81F3
Limoges *France* 69C2
Limón *Costa Rica* 25C5
Limousin Province *France* 69C2
Linares *Spain* 73B2
Lincang *China* 117E4
Lincoln Reg *USA* 55G4
Lincoln *USA* 17D1
Linfen *China* 114F3
Linköping *Sweden* 94D4
Linosa I. *Italy* 79C3
Linz *Aust.* 91C3
Lipari I. *Italy* 79C3

Place	Ref
Lisbon Port.	73A2
Lisburn N.Ire.	65E2
Lisieux France	68C2
Little Rock USA	18D2
Liuzhou China	117E4
Livanátais Greece	80E3
Liverpool Eng	53E4
Livingston Scot	63E5
Livingstone Zambia	148C2
Livno Bos.Herz	77D2
Livorno Italy	76C2
Ljubljana Slovenia	77C1
Llandrindod Wells Wales	58D5
Lobito Angola	148B2
Lochboisdale Scot	60A3
Lochgilphead Scot	62C4
Lochinver Scot	60C2
Lochmaddy Scot	60A3
Locri Italy	79D3
Lódź Pol.	86D2
Logroño Spain	72B1
Loja Ecuador	35B3
Loja Spain	73B2
Lolland I. Den.	94C5
Lom Bulg.	82E2
Lombok I. Indon.	123D4
Lome Togo	145D2
London Eng	56G6
Londonderry N.Ire.	65D1
Long Island The Bahamas	26E2
Long Island I. USA	19F1
Longford Ireland	67D3
Lorca Spain	75B2
Lord Howe I. Aust.	157F4
Lorient France	68B2
Los Angeles USA	16B2
Los Mochis Mexico	23C3
Losinj I. Yugos.	63E5
Louisiana State USA	20D2
Louisville USA	18E2
Loukhi Russia	93G2
Louth Eng	55G4
Loznica Yugos.	82D2
Lu'an China	114F3
Luanda Angola	148B1
Luang Prabang Laos	118C2
Lubango Angola	148B2
Lubbock USA	17C2
Lübeck FRG	85C2
Lublin Pol.	88E2
Lubumbashi Dem. Rep. of Congo	148C2
Lucca Italy	76C2
Lucknow India	127G3
Lüda China	112G3
Lüderitz Namibia	149B3
Ludhiana India	126F2
Ludvika Sweden	94D3
Luga Russia	95F4
Lugo Spain	72A1
Luleå Sweden	58C6
Lundy I. Eng	58C6
Luohe China	114F3
Luoyang China	114F3
Lurgan N.Ire.	65E2
Lusaka Zambia	148C2
Luton Eng	56G6
Luxembourg Lux.	70D2
Luxor Egypt	142G2
Luzern Switz.	70D2
Luzhou China	117E4
Luzon I. Phil.	120E2
L'viv Ukraine	102D5
Lybster Scot	61E2
Lycksele Sweden	93D3
Lyon France	71C2

M

Place	Ref
Maastricht Neth	90B2
Ma'ān Jordan	130B2
Macapá Brazil	36D2
Macau China	119D1
Macclesfield Eng	53E4
Maceió Brazil	37F3
Mackay Aust.	156D3
Macomer Sardegna	78B2
Mâcon France	71C2
Macon USA	20E2
Macquarie I. NZ	165
Madang PNG	125G4
Madeira I. Atlantic O.	140B3
Madison USA	18E1
Madras (Chennai) India	129G4
Madrid Spain	72B1
Madura I. Indon.	123D4
Madurai India	128F5
Mafia I. Tanz.	150D1
Mafikeng S.Africa	149C34
Magadan Russia	105R4
Magdeburg FRG	85C2
Magnitogorsk Russia	109G4
Mahajanga Madag.	150E3
Mahalapye Botswana	149C3
Mahón Spain	74C2
Maidstone Eng	56H6
Maiduguri Nig.	145E3
Maine Province France	68B2
Maine State USA	19F1
Mainland I. Scot Orkney I.	61J7
Mainland I. Scot Shetland I.	61E1
Mainz FRG	90E3
Maitland Aust.	157E4
Maizuru Japan	115L9
Majene Indon.	123D4
Majorca I. Spain	74C2
Makarska Cro.	77D2
Makhachkala Russia	108F5
Makkah S.Arabia	132B3
Makó Hung.	88B3
Makurdi Nig.	145D2
Malabo Bioko I.	145D2
Malaga Spain	73B2
Malakal Sudan	146A4
Malang Indon.	123D4
Malanje Angola	148B1
Malatya Turk.	130B2
Malden I. Kiribati	162
Maldives Is. Indian O.	128F5
Malekula I. Vanuatu	156F2
Mallaig Scot	60C3
Mallow Ireland	66C4
Malmö Sweden	94C4
Malton Eng	55G3
Mamou Guinea	144A1
Man Cote d'Ivoire	144B2
Mana Hawaiian Is.	22H
Manacor Spain	74C2
Manado Indon.	124E3
Managua Nic.	25B4
Manakara Madag.	151E3
Manaus Brazil	35C3
Manchester Eng	53E4
Mandal Nor.	94B4
Mandalay Myanmar	118B1
Mangalia Rom.	83F2
Mangalore India	128F4
Manila Phil.	120E2
Manitoba State Canada	13H4
Manizales Colombia	34B2
Mannheim FRG	90B3
Manokwari Indon.	124F4
Mansfield Eng	55F4
Manta Ecuador	34A3
Mantes France	68C2
Manzanillo Cuba	24D2
Manzhouli China	112F2
Maoming China	114F4
Maputo Mozam.	151D3
Maracaibo Ven.	34B1
Maradi Niger	145D1
Maranhão State Brazil	37E3
Marbella Spain	73B2
Marburg FRG	90B2
Mardan Pak.	126F2
Mar del Plata Arg.	38E6
Margate Eng	56J6
Maribor Cro.	77D1
Marie-Galánte I. Caribbean Sea	26G3
Mariestad Sweden	94C4
Marília Brazil	38F5
Marmaris Turkey	81F3
Marne France	68B2
Marquises Is. Pacific O.	162
Marrakech Mor.	140C3
Marseille France	71D3
Marshall Is. Pacific O.	159
Martinique I. Caribbean Sea	27G4
Mary Turkmenistan	108H6
Maryland State USA	19F2
Masaya Nic.	25B4
Masbate I. Phil.	120E2
Maseru Lesotho	149C3
Mashhad Iran	131D2
Masirah I. Oman	133D3
Masqat Oman	133D3
Massa Italy	76C2
Massachusetts State USA	19F1
Matadi Dem Rep. of Congo	148B3
Matagalpa Nic.	25B4
Matamoros Mexico	23D3
Matanzas Cuba	24C2
Mataram Indon.	123D4
Matlock Eng	55F4
Mato Grosso Do Sul State	37D4
Mato Grosso State Brazil	37D4
Matsue Japan	113H3
Matsumoto Japan	115M8
Matsusaka Japan	115M9
Matsuyama Japan	113H3
Maui Hawaiian Is.	22H
Mauritius I. Indian O.	151F4
Mayagüana I. The Bahamas	26E2
Maybole Scot	62D5
Mayotte I. Indian O.	150E2
Mazár-e Sharif Afghan.	126E2

Mazatlán *Mexico*	23C3
Mbabane *Swaziland*	151D3
Mbandaka	
Dem. Rep. of Congo	146E4
Mbarara *Uganda*	146G5
Mbeya *Tanz.*	150D1
Mbuji-Mayi	
Dem.Rep. of Congo	146F5
Meaux *France*	70C2
Medan *Indon.*	122B3
Medellín *Colombia*	34B2
Medgidia *Rom.*	83F2
Medicine Hat *Canada*	13G4
Meerut *India*	126F3
Meiktila *Myanmar*	118B1
Meknés *Mor.*	140C3
Melaka *Malay.*	122C3
Melbourne *Aust.*	157D4
Melilla *Spain*	73B2
Melitopol' *Ukraine*	108E5
Melo *Urug.*	38E6
Melun *France*	70C2
Melvich *Scot*	61E2
Melville I. *Aust.*	154C2
Melville I. *Canada*	12G2
Melville Pen. *Canada*	14D3
Memphis *USA*	18E2
Mende *France*	71C3
Mendoza *Arg.*	40C6
Mendoza State *Arg.*	40C6
Menongue *Angola*	148C2
Menzanares *Spain*	73B2
Merauke *Indon.*	125G4
Mercedes *Arg.*	40C6
Mergui Arch. *Myanmar*	118B2
Mérida *Mexico*	20E3
Mérida *Spain*	73A2
Merthyr Tydfil *Wales*	58D6
Mesolóngian *Greece*	80E3
Messina *Italy*	79D3
Metz *France*	70D2
Mexicali *USA*	16B2
México *Mexico*	23D4
Meymaneh *Afghan.*	126E2
Miami *USA*	21E3
Mianyany *China*	117E3
Michigan State *USA*	18E1
Michurin *Bulg.*	83F2
Midway Is. *Pacific O.*	159
Mikkeli *Fin*	95F3
Mikonos I. *Greece*	81F3
Milano *Italy*	76B1
Mildura *Aust.*	155D4
Milford Haven *Wales*	58B6
Millau *France*	71C3
Milos *Greece*	81E3
Milton Keynes *Eng*	56G5
Milwaukee *USA*	18E1
Minas Gerais State *Brazil*	37E4
Minatinán *Mexico*	20D4
Mindanao *Phil.*	120E3
Mindoro I. *Phil.*	120E2
Minna *Nig.*	145D2
Minneapolis *USA*	18D1
Minnesota State *USA*	17D1
Minorca I. *Spain*	74C2
Minsk *Belarus*	102D4
Miranda de Ebro *Spain*	72B1
Miri *Malay.*	123D3

Mirzapur *India*	127G3
Misiones State *Arg.*	38E5
Miskolc *Hung.*	88E3
Misool *Indon.*	124F4
Misrâtah *Libya*	141E3
Mississippi State *USA*	20D2
Missouri State *USA*	18D2
Mito *Japan*	115P8
Miyako *Japan*	115P7
Miyazaki *Japan*	115H3
Mizusawa *Japan*	115P7
Mjölby *Sweden*	94D4
Mlawa *Pol.*	86E2
Mljet I. *Cro.*	82D2
M. Lampang *Thai*	118B2
M. Nakhon Sawan *Thai.*	118C2
Mo-i-Rana *Nor.*	92C2
Mobile *USA*	20E2
Moçambique *Mozam.*	150E2
Modena *Italy*	77C2
Moffat *Scot*	63E5
Mogadishu *Somalia*	147H4
Mogilev *Belurus*	102E4
Mokp'o *S.Korea*	112G3
Molde *Nor.*	92B3
Mollendo *Peru*	35B4
Molokai I. *Hawaiian Is.*	22H
Mombasa *Kenya*	147G5
Monaco *Monaco*	71D3
Monaghan *Ireland*	65E2
Mondovi *Italy*	76B2
Mongu *Zambia*	148C2
Monopoli *Italy*	79D2
Monreal del Campo *Spain*	74B1
Monrovia *Lib.*	144A2
Montana State *USA*	17B1
Montargis *France*	70C2
Montauban *France*	69C3
Montbéliard *France*	70D2
Monte Cristi *Haiti*	26E3
Montego Bay *Jamaica*	24D3
Monteria *Colombia*	34B2
Monterrey *Mexico*	23C3
Montes Claros *Brazil*	37E4
Montevideo *Urug.*	38E6
Montgomery *USA*	20E2
Montluçon *France*	71C2
Montpelier *USA*	19F1
Montréal *Canada*	15L5
Montrose *Scot*	63F4
Montserrat I. *Caribbean Sea*	26G3
Monza *Italy*	76B1
Mopti *Mali*	144B1
Mora *Sweden*	94C3
Moradabad *India*	126F3
Morioka *Japan*	115P7
Moroni *Comoros*	150E2
Morotai I. *Indon.*	124E3
Morwell *Aust.*	157D4
Moshi *Tanz.*	147G5
Mosjöen *Nor.*	92C2
Moskva *Russia*	105E4
Moss *Nor.*	94C4
Mossoró *Brazil*	37F3
Mostaganem *Alg.*	141D3
Mostar *Bos.Herz.*	82D2
Motherwell *Scot*	63E5
Motril *Spain*	73B2

Moulins *France*	71C2
Moulmein *Myanmar*	118B2
Moundou *Chad*	145E4
Mount Gambier *Aust.*	155D4
Mount Isa *Aust.*	154C3
M. Phitsanulok *Thai.*	118C2
Mt. Magnet *Aust.*	155A3
Mtwara *Tanz.*	150E2
Mudanjiang *China*	112G2
Mufulira *Zambia*	148C2
Muhos *Fin*	93F3
Mulhouse *France*	70D2
Mull I. *Scot*	62C4
Mullingar *Ireland*	67D3
Multan *Pak.*	126F2
Mumbai (Bombay)*India*	124E4
Muna I. *Indon.*	124E4
München *FRG*	91C3
Mungbere	
Dem. Rep. of Congo	146F4
Munster *FRG*	84B2
Muonio *Fin*	93E2
Muqhisho *Somalia*	147H4
Murcia *Spain*	75B2
Murcia Region *Spain*	75B2
Murmansk *Russia*	103E3
Musselburgh *Scot*	63E5
Mutare *Zim.*	151D2
Mwanza *Tanz.*	146F5
Mwene Ditu	
Dem. Rep of Congo	146F5
My Tho *Viet.*	119C2
Myingyan *Myanmar*	118B1
Myitkyina *Myanmar*	118B1
Mymensingh *Bang.*	127H3
Mysore *India*	128F4

N

Naas *Ireland*	67E3
Naga *Phil.*	120E2
Nagano *Japan*	115N8
Nagaoka *Japan*	115N8
Nagasaki *Japan*	115G3
Nagercoil *India*	128F5
Nagoya *Japan*	115M9
Nagpur *India*	128F3
Nagykanizsa *Hung.*	91D3
Nain *Canada*	15M4
Nairn *Scot*	61E3
Nairobi *Kenya*	147G5
Nakhodka *Russia*	107P5
Nakhon Ratchasima *Thai.*	118C2
Nakhon Si Thammarat *Thai.*118B3	
Nakuru *Kenya*	147G5
Nam Dinh *Viet.*	119C1
Namangan *Uzbekistan*	109J5
Namibe *Angola*	148B2
Nampula *Mozam.*	150D2
Nanchang *China*	114F4
Nanchong *China*	117E3
Nancy *France*	70D2
Nanjing *China*	114F3
Nanning *China*	117E4
Nanping *China*	114F4
Nantes *France*	68B2
Nantong *China*	114G3
Nanyang *China*	114F3
Napoli *Italy*	79C2
Narbonne *France*	71C3

Narva *Estonia*	95F4
Narvik *Nor.*	92D2
Nar'yan Mar *Russia*	103G3
Nashville *USA*	18E2
Nassau *The Bahamas*	24D1
Natal *Brazil*	37F3
Natuna Besar *I. Indon.*	123C3
Navarra Region *Spain*	74B1
Náxos I. *Greece*	81F3
Ndjamena *Chad*	145E3
Ndola *Zambia*	148C2
Neápolos *Greece*	81E3
Near Islands *USA*	22J
Nebraska State *USA*	17C1
Negros *Phil.*	120E3
Nei Mongol Zizhiqu Provin *China*	112F2
Neiva *Colombia*	34B2
Nellore *India*	129G4
Nelson *Eng*	53E4
Nelson *NZ*	157G5
Nenagh *Ireland*	66C4
Neubrandenburg *FRG*	85C2
Neumünster *FRG*	85B2
Neuquén *Arg.*	40C6
Neuquén State *Arg.*	40C6
Nevada State *USA*	16B2
Nevers *France*	70C2
Newark *USA*	19F1
Newark-on-Trent *Eng*	55G4
New Britain I. *Pacific O.*	125G4
New Brunswick *Canada*	15M5
Newcastle *Aust.*	157E4
Newcastle-upon-Tyne *Eng*	54F3
New Delhi *India*	126F3
Newfoundland *Canada*	15M4
New Georgia *Solomon Is.*	156E1
New Hampshire State *USA*	19F1
New Jersey State *USA*	19F1
New Mexico State *USA*	17C2
New Orleans *USA*	20E3
Newport *Isle of Wight*	57F7
Newport *Wales*	58E6
Newquay *Eng*	59B7
New Ross *Ireland*	67E4
Newry *N.Ire.*	65E2
New South Wales State *Aust.*	157D4
Newton Aycliffe *Eng*	54F3
Newton Stewart *Scot*	62D6
Newtown-abbey *N.Ire.*	65F2
New York *USA*	19F1
New York State *USA*	18F1
Ngaoundéré *Cameroon*	145E4
Nguru *Nig.*	145E3
Nha Trang *Viet.*	119C2
Niamey *Niger*	144B3
Nias I. *Indon.*	122B4
Nice *France*	71D3
Nicobar I. *India*	129H5
Nicosia *Cyprus*	130B2
Niigata *Japan*	115N8
Nijmegen *Neth.*	84B2
Nikel *Russia*	93G2
Nikolayev *Russia*	108E5
Nîmes *France*	71C3
Ningbo *China*	114G4
Ningxia Province *China*	111E3
Nioro du Sahel *Mali*	140C5

Niort *France*	69B2
Niš *Yugos.*	82E2
Nitra *Slovakia.*	88D3
Niue I. *Pacific O.*	165
Nivernais Province *France*	70C2
Nizamabad *India*	128F4
Nizhny Novgorod *Russia*	108F4
Nizhniy Tagil *Russia*	109H4
Nkongsamba *Cameroon*	145D2
Nong Khai *Thai.*	118C2
Norfolk *USA*	19F2
Norfolk I. *Aust.*	157F3
Noril'sk *Russia*	103K3
Normandie Province *France*	68B2
Norrköping *Sweden*	94D4
Norseman *Aust.*	155B4
North Bay *Canada*	15L5
North Carolina State *USA*	18E2
North Dakota State *USA*	17C1
Northern Mariana I. *Pacific O.*	121G2
Northern Ter. State *Aust.*	154C2
North I. *NZ*	157G4
North Uist I. *Scot*	60A3
Northwest Territories State *Canada*	12G3
Norwich *Eng*	56J5
Notodden *Nor.*	94B4
Nottingham *Eng*	55F5
Nouadhibou *Maur.*	140B4
Nouakchott *Maur.*	140B5
Nouméa *Nouvelle Calédonie*	156E1
Nouvelle Calédonie I. *Pacific O.*	156E1
Novara *Italy*	76B1
Nova Scotia *Canada*	15M5
Novaya Zemlya *Russia*	103G2
Novi Pazar *Yugos.*	82E2
Novi Sad *Yugos.*	82D1
Novokuznatsk *Russia*	109K4
Novorossysk *Russia*	108E5
Novosibirsk *Russia*	109K4
Novosibirskiye Ostrova I. *Russia*	104Q2
N. Ronaldsay I. *Scot*	61F1
Nuku'alofa *Tonga*	165
Nukus *Uzbekistan*	108G5
Numazu *Japan*	115N9
Nunivak I. *USA*	12B3
Nürnberg *FRG*	91B3
Nyala *Sudan*	146F3
Nyíregyháza *Hung.*	88E3
Nyköping *Sweden*	94D4
Nyngan *Aust.*	157D4
Nzérékoré *Guinea*	144B2

O

Oahu I. *Hawaiian Is.*	22H
Oban *Scot*	62C4
Obi I. *Indon.*	124E4
Odawara *Japan*	115N9
Odda *Nor.*	94B3
Odemira *Port.*	83A2
Odense *Den.*	94C4
Odessa *Ukraine*	108D5
Odessa *USA*	23C2
Offenbach *FRG*	90B2
Ōgaki *Japan*	115M9

Ogasawara-Shotó *Jap.*	121G1
Ogbomosho *Nig.*	145D2
Ogden *USA*	17B1
Ohrid *Macedonia*	80E2
Okaya *Japan*	115N8
Okayama *Japan*	113H3
Okazaki *Japan*	115M9
Okehampton *Eng*	59C7
Okhotsk *Russia*	105Q4
Okinawa I. *Japan*	113G4
Oklahoma City *USA*	17D2
Oklahoma State *USA*	17D2
Öland I. *Sweden*	94D4
Olbia *Sardegna*	78B2
Oldenburg *FRG*	84B2
Olomouc *Czech.Rep.*	91D3
Olsztyn *Pol.*	86E2
Olympia *USA*	16A1
Omagh *N.Ire.*	65D2
Omaha *USA*	17D1
Omdurman *Sudan*	142G3
Omsk *Russia*	109J4
Onitsha *Nig.*	145D2
Ontario State *Canada*	15J4
Oostende *Belg.*	70C1
Opole *Pol.*	88D2
Oppdal *Nor.*	92B3
Oradea *Rom.*	88E3
Oran *Alg.*	141C3
Orange *Aust.*	157D4
Orange *France*	71C3
Orbetello *Italy*	77C2
Oléanais Province *France*	68C2
Örebro *Sweden*	94D4
Oregon State *USA*	16A1
Orel *Russia*	108E4
Orenburg *Russia*	108G4
Orénse *Spain*	72A1
Oristano *Sardegna*	78B3
Orkney Is. *Scot*	61E1
Orlando *USA*	20E3
Orléans *France*	68C2
Örnsköldsvik *Sweden*	93D3
Orsk *Russia*	109G4
Oruro *Bolivia*	35C4
Ōsaka *Japan*	155L9
Oshogbo *Nig.*	145D2
Osijek *Cro.*	82D1
Oskarshamn *Sweden*	94D4
Oslo *Nor.*	94C4
Osnabrück *FRG*	84B2
Osorno *Chile*	41B7
Östersund *Sweden*	92C3
Ostia *Italy*	77C2
Ostrava *Czech. Rep.*	88D3
Oswestry *Eng*	53D5
Otaru *Japan*	113J2
Ottawa *Canada*	15L5
Ouagadougou *Burkina Faso*	144C3
Ouahigouya *Burkina Faso*	144B1
Ouargla *Alg.*	141D3
Oudtshoorn *S.Africa*	149C4
Oujda *Mor.*	141C3
Oulu *Fin*	93F2
Outer Hebrides *Scot*	60A3
Oviedo *Spain*	72A1
Oxford *Eng*	56F6
Oyem *Gabon*	145E4

P

Padang *Indon.*	122C4
Paderborn *FRG*	84B2
Pag I. *Cro.*	77D2
Pagai Selatan I. *Indon.*	123C4
Pagai Utara I. *Indon.*	122B4
Pahala *Hawaiian Is.*	22H
Pais Vasco Region *Spain*	72B1
Paisley *Scot*	62D5
Palan i. *Pacific O.*	158
Palangkaraya *Indon.*	123D4
Palau Caroline Is.	124F3
Palawan I. *Phil.*	120D2
Palembang *Indon.*	122C4
Palencia *Spain*	72B1
Palermo *Italy*	79C3
Palma de Mallorca *Spain*	74C2
Palmerston North *NZ*	157G5
Palmi *Italy*	79D3
Palmyra *Pacific O.*	160
Palu *Indon.*	123D4
Pamplona *Spain*	74B1
Panamá *Panama*	25D5
Panay I. *Phil.*	120E2
Pangkalpinang *Indon.*	123D4
Pantelleria I. *Italy*	78C3
Papa Westray I. *Scot*	61F1
Pará State *Brazil*	37D3
Paracel I. *S.China Sea*	119D2
Paracin *Yugos.*	82E2
Paraiba State *Brazil*	37F3
Parakou *Benin*	145D2
Paramaribo *Suriname*	36D2
Paraná *Arg.*	40C6
Parana State *Brazil*	38E5
Parepare *Indon.*	123D4
Paris *France*	68C2
Parkano *Fin*	95E3
Parma *Italy*	76C2
Parnaiba *Brazil*	37E3
Pärnu *Estonia*	95E4
Pasadena *USA*	16B2
Passo Fundo *Brazil*	38E5
Pasto *Colombia*	34B2
Patna *India*	127G3
Pátrai *Greece*	80E3
Pau *France*	69B3
Pavlodar *Kazakhstan*	109J4
P.Dolak I. *Indon.*	125F4
Pec *Yugos.*	82E2
Pécs *Hung.*	88D3
Peebles *Scot*	63E5
Pegu *Myanmar*	118B2
Pekanbaru *Indon.*	122C3
Peking (Beijing) *China*	112F3
Pello *Fin*	93E2
Pelopónnisos I. *Greece*	80E3
Pemba *Mozam.*	150E2
Pemba I. *Tanz.*	147G5
Pembroke *Wales*	58C6
Pennsylvania State *USA*	18F1
Penrith *Eng*	52E3
Penza *Russia*	108F4
Penzance *Eng*	59B7
Pereira *Colombia*	34B2
Périgueux *France*	69C2
Perm *Russia*	109G4
Pernambuco State *Brazil*	37F3

Perpignan *France*	71C3
Perth *Aust.*	155A4
Perth *Scot*	62E4
Perugia *Italy*	77C2
Pescara *Italy*	77C2
Peshawar *Pak.*	126F2
Peterborough *Eng*	56G5
Peterhead *Scot*	61G3
Petropavlovsk *Kazakhstan*	109H4
Petropavlovsk Kamchatskiy *Russia*	105R4
Petrozavodsk *Russia*	102E3
Philadelphia *USA*	19F1
Phnom Penh *Camb.*	119C2
Phoenix *USA*	16B2
Phoenix Is. *Kiribati*	165
Phuket I. *Thai.*	118B3
Piacenza *Italy*	76B1
Piaui State *Brazil*	37E3
Picardie Province *France*	70C2
Pierre *USA*	17C1
Pietermaritzburg *S.Africa*	149D3
Pietersburg *S.Africa*	149C3
Pila *Pol.*	85D2
Pilos *Greece*	80E3
Pinar del Rio *Cuba*	24C2
Pingliang *China*	117E3
Piombino *Italy*	76C2
Piraiévs *Greece*	81E3
Pírgos *Greece*	80E3
Pirot *Yugos.*	82E2
Pisa *Italy*	76C2
Pitcairn I. *Pacific O.*	162
Piteå *Sweden*	93E2
Pitesti *Rom.*	83E2
Pitlochry *Scot*	62E4
Pittsburgh *USA*	18F1
Piura *Peru*	35A3
Plasencia *Spain*	72A1
Pleven *Bulg.*	83E2
Ploiesti *Rom.*	83F2
Plovdiv *Bulg.*	83E2
Plymouth *Eng*	59C7
Plzen *Czech.*	91C3
Podgorica *Yugos.*	82D2
Pointe-à-Pitre *Guadeloup*	26G3
Pointe Noire *Congo*	145E3
Poitiers *France*	69C2
Poitou Province *France*	69B2
Polla *Italy*	79D2
Poltava *Ukraine*	108E5
Ponce *Puerto Rico*	26F3
Ponferrada *Spain*	72A1
Pontevedra *Spain*	72A1
Pontianak *Indon.*	123C4
Poole *Eng*	57F7
Pori *Fin*	95E3
Port Augusta *Aust.*	155C4
Port au Prince *Haiti*	26E3
Port Elizabeth *S.Africa*	149C4
Port Gentil *Gabon*	145D3
Port Harcourt *Nig.*	145D2
Port Headland *Aust.*	154A3
Portland *USA*	16A
Port Laoise *Ireland*	67D3
Port Louis *Mauritius*	151F4
Port Moresby *PNG*	125G4
Pôrto Alegre *Brazil*	38E5
Port of Spain *Trinidad*	27G4

Porto Novo *Benin*	145D2
Porto *Port.*	72A1
Porto Torres *Sardegna*	78B2
Porto Vecchio *Corse*	76B2
Pôrto Velho *Brazil*	35C3
Port Pirie *Aust.*	155C4
Port Said *Egypt*	142G1
Portsmouth *Eng*	57F7
Port Sudan *Sudan*	143G3
Port Talbot *Wales*	58D6
Poso *Indon.*	124E4
Potchefstroom *S.Africa*	149C3
Potenza *Italy*	79D2
Potosi *Bolivia*	35C4
Potsdam *FRG*	85C2
Poznan *Pol.*	85D2
Prato *Italy*	77C2
Preston *Eng*	53E4
Preswick *Scot*	62D5
Pretoria *S.Africa*	149C3
Prince Edward I. *Can.*	15M5
Prince George *Canada*	13F4
Prince of Wales I. *Canada*	12H2
Prince Rupert *Canada*	13F4
Principe I. *W.Africa*	145D2
Pristina *Czech.*	82E2
Prokop'yevsk *Russia*	109K4
Prome *Myanmar*	118B2
Provence Province *France*	71D3
Providence *USA*	19F1
Prudhoe Bay *USA*	12D2
Przemys'l *Pol.*	88E3
Pskov *Russia*	102D4
Pucallpa *Peru*	35B3
Puebla *Mexico*	23D4
Puerto Armuelles *Panama*	25C5
Puerto Ayacucho *Ven.*	34C2
Puerto Barrios *Guatemala*	25B3
Puerto Cabezas *Nic.*	25C4
Puerto Cortés *Honduras*	25B4
Puerto Juárez *Mexico*	20E3
Puerto Montt *Chile*	41B7
Puerto Plata *Dom. Republic*	26E3
Puerto Rico I. *Caribbean*	26F3
Puertollano *Spain*	73B2
Pula *Cro.*	77C2
Pune *India*	128F4
Punta Arenas *Chile*	41B8
Puntarenas *Costa Rica*	25C5
Pusan *S.Korea*	113G3
Puttgarden *FRG*	85C2
Pyŏngyang *China*	112G3

Q

Qamdo *China*	117D3
Qazvin *Iran*	131C2
Qena *Egypt*	142G2
Qingdao *China*	112G3
Qinghai Province *China*	111D3
Qingjiang *China*	114F3
Qinhuangdao *China*	112F2
Qiqihar *China*	112G2
Qom *Iran*	131D2
Qu Xian *China*	114F4
Quanzhou *China*	114F4
Québec *Canada*	15L5
Québec State *Canada*	15L4
Queen Charlotte Is. *Can*	13E4

Place	Ref.
Queen Elizabeth Is. *Can*	12G2
Queensland State *Aust.*	154D3
Quelimane *Mozam.*	150D2
Quetta *Pak.*	126E3
Quezaltenango *Guatemala*	25A4
Quezon City *Phil.*	120E2
Qui Nhon *Viet.*	119C2
Quilon *India*	128F5
Quimper *France*	68B2
Quito *Ecuador*	34B3
R	
Raasay I. *Scot*	60B3
Rab I. *Cro.*	77C2
Raba *Indon.*	123D4
Rabat *Mor.*	140C3
Radom *Pol.*	88E2
Raipur *India*	129G3
Rajkot *India*	128F3
Raleigh *USA*	18F2
Ramsey *Isle of Man*	53C3
Rancagua *Chile*	40B6
Randers *Den.*	94C4
Rangpur *Bang.*	127G3
Rapid City *USA*	17C1
Rasht *Iran*	131C2
Ráth Luirc *Ireland*	66C4
Rathlin I. *N.Ire.*	65E1
Ratlam *India*	128F3
Rauma *Fin*	95E3
Ravenna *Italy*	77C2
Rawalpindi *Pak.*	126F2
Razgrad *Bulg.*	83F2
Reading *Eng*	56G6
Recife *Brazil*	37F3
Redon *France*	68B2
Regensburg *FRG*	91B3
Reggane *Alg.*	141D4
Reggio di Calabria *Italy*	79D3
Reggio nell'Emilia *Italy*	76C2
Regina *Canada*	13H4
Reims *France*	70C2
Renell I. *Solomon Is.*	156F2
Rennes *France*	68B2
Reno *USA*	16B2
Resistencia *Arg.*	40D5
Resolution I. *Canada*	14M3
Réunion I. *Indian O.*	151F4
Reykjavik *Iceland*	92A2
Rhode Island State *USA*	19F1
Rhodes I. *Greece*	81F3
Rhum I. *Scot*	62B4
Rhyl *Wales*	53E4
Richmond *USA*	19F2
Riga *Latvia*	102D4
Rijeka *Cro.*	77C2
Rimini *Italy*	77C2
Rîmnicu Vîlcea *Rom.*	89E3
Ringwood *Eng*	57F7
Rio Branco *Brazil*	35C3
Rio de Janeiro *Brazil*	38F5
Rio de Janeiro State *Brazil*	38F5
Rio Gallegos *Arg.*	41C8
Rio Grande *Arg.*	38E5
Rio Grande do Norte State *Brazil*	37F3
Rio Grande do Sul State *Brazil*	38E5
Rio Negro State *Arg.*	41C7
Ripon *Eng*	55F3
Roanne *France*	71C2
Rochdale *Eng*	53E4
Rochester *Eng*	56H6
Rochester *USA*	18D1
Rockford *USA*	18E1
Rockhampton *Aust.*	156E3
Rødbyhavn *Den.*	94C5
Ródhos *Greece*	81F3
Roman *Rom.*	89F3
Rome *Italy*	77C2
Ronda *Spain*	73A2
Rondônia State *Brazil*	35C4
Rosario *Arg.*	40C6
Roscoff *France*	68B2
Roscommon *Ireland*	66C3
Roscrea *Ireland*	67D4
Roseau *Dominica*	27G3
Rosslare *Ireland*	67E4
Rostock *FRG*	85C2
Rostov-na-Donu *Russia*	108E5
Rotherham *Eng*	55F4
Rotterdam *Neth.*	84A2
Roti I. *Indon.*	124E5
Rouen *France*	68C2
Round I. *Mauritius*	151F4
Rousay I. *Scot*	61E1
Roussillon Province *France*	69C3
Rovaniemi *Fin*	93F2
Royal Tunbridge Wells *Eng*	56H6
Ruffec *France*	69C2
Rugby *Eng*	56F5
Rugen I. *FRG*	85C2
Ruma *Yugos.*	82D1
Runcorn *Eng*	53E4
Ruoqiang *China*	110C3
Ruse *Bulg.*	83F2
Ruteng *Indon.*	124E4
Ryazan' *Russia*	108E4
Rybinsk *Rus.*	102E4
Rybnik *Pol.*	88D2
Ryūkyū Is. *Japan*	113G4
Rzeszów *Pol.*	88E2
S	
Saarbrucken *FRG*	90B3
Saaremaa I. *Est.*	95E4
Sabac *Yugos.*	82D2
Sabadell *Spain*	74C1
Sabhá *Libya*	141E4
Sacramento *USA*	16A2
Sadiya *India*	127H3
Safi *Mor.*	140C3
Sagunto *Spain*	74B2
Saintes *France*	69B2
Sakai *Japan*	115L9
Sakata *Japan*	115N7
Sakhalin I. *Russia*	107Q4
Sakishima guntō *Japan*	115G4
Salālah *Oman*	133D4
Salamanca *Spain*	72A1
Salangen *Nor.*	92D2
Salayar I. *Indon.*	124E4
Salbris *France*	68C2
Salem *India*	128F4
Salem *USA*	16A1
Salerno *Italy*	79C2
Salford *Eng*	53E4
Salisbury *Eng*	56F6
Salo *Fin*	95E3
Salonta *Rom.*	82B1
Salt Lake City *USA*	17B1
Salta *Arg.*	40C5
Salta State *Arg.*	40C5
Saltillo *Mexico*	23C3
Salto *Urug.*	40D6
Salvador *Brazil*	37F4
Salzburg *Aust.*	91C3
Salzgitter-Bad *FRG*	85C2
Samar I. *Phil.*	120E2
Samara *Russia*	108G4
Samarinda *Indon.*	123D4
Samarkand *Uzbekistan*	109H6
Sámos I. *Greece*	81F3
Samothráki I. *Greece*	81F2
Samsun *Turk.*	130B1
San *Mali*	144B1
San Antonio *USA*	23D3
San'a *Rep.Yemen*	132C4
San Benedetto del Tronto *Italy*	77C2
San Cristóbal *Ven.*	34B2
San Cristobal I. *Solomon Is.*	156F2
Sancti Spíritus *Cuba*	24D2
Sandakan *Malay.*	123D3
Sanday I. *Scot*	61F1
San Diego *USA*	16B2
San Fernando *Phil.*	120E2
San Francisco *USA*	16A2
Sanjō *Japan*	115N8
San José *Costa Rica*	25C5
San Jose *USA*	16A2
San Juan *Arg.*	40C6
San Juan *Puerto Rico*	26F3
San Juan del Norte *Nic.*	25C4
San Juan del Sur *Nic.*	25B4
San Juan State *Arg.*	40C6
San Julián *Arg.*	41C7
San Luis Potosi *Mexico*	23C3
San Luis *Arg.*	40C6
San Luis State *Arg.*	40C6
Sanmenxia *China*	114F3
San Marino *San Marino*	77D2
San Miguel de Tucuman *Arg.*	40C5
San Miguel *El Sal.*	25B4
San Pedro Sula *Honduras*	25B3
San Remo *Italy*	76B2
San Salvador *El Sal.*	25B4
San Salvador I. *The Bahamas*	26E1
San Sebastian *Spain*	74B1
Santa Ana *El Sal.*	25B4
Santa Catarina State *Brazil*	38E5
Santa Clara *Cuba*	24C2
Santa Cruz *Bolivia*	35C4
Santa Cruz Is. *Solomon Is.*	156F2
Santa Cruz State *Arg.*	41B7
Santa Fé *USA*	17C2
Santa Fe State *Arg.*	40C5
Santa Isabel I. *Solomon Is.*	156E1
Santa Marta *Colombia*	34B1
Santander *Spain*	72B1
Santarém *Brazil*	37D3
Santarém *Port.*	73A2
Santa Rosa *Arg.*	40C5
Santa State *Arg.*	40C5
Santiago *Chile*	40B6

Santiago *Dom. Republic* 26E3
Santiago *Panama* 25C5
Santiago de Compostela
  Spain 72A1
Santiago de Cuba *Cuba* 24D3
Santiago del Estero State
  Arg. 40C5
Santo Domingo
  Dom. Republic 26F3
São Carlos *Brazil* 38F5
São Luis *Brazil* 37E3
São Paulo *Brazil* 38F5
São Paulo State *Brazil* 38F5
São Tomé *I.W.Africa* 145D2
São Tomé and PríncipeRep.
  W.Africa 145D2
Sapporo *Japan* 113J2
Sapri *Italy* 79D2
Sarajevo *Bos.Herz.* 82D2
Saratov *Russia* 108F4
Sardegna *Italy* 78B2
Sarh *Chad* 146E4
Sark I. *UK* 59E8
Sarrion *Spain* 74B1
Sasebo *Japan* 115G3
Saskatchewan State
  Canada 13H4
Saskatoon *Canada* 13H4
Sassandra Côte d'Ivoire* 144B2
Sassari *Sardegna* 78B2
Sassnitz *FRG* 85C2
Satu Mare *Rom.* 88E3
Sault Ste Marie *Canada* 15K5
Savannah *USA* 20E2
Savannakhet *Laos.* 119C2
Savoie Province *France* 71D2
Savona *Italy* 76B2
Savonlinna *Fin* 93F3
Saxmundham *Eng* 56J5
Saynshand *Mongolia* 112F2
Scarborough *Eng* 55G3
Schwerin *FRG* 85C2
Scourie *Scot* 60C2
Scunthorpe *Eng* 55G4
Seattle *USA* 16A1
Seaward Pen. *USA* 12B3
Sebes *Rom.* 88E3
Ségou *Mali* 144B1
Segovia *Spain* 72B1
Seinäjoki *Fin* 93E3
Sekondi *Ghana* 145C4
Selby *Eng* 55F4
Semarang *Indon.* 123D4
Semipalatinsk *Kazakhstan* 109K4
Sendai *Japan* 115P7
Senlis *France* 70C2
Sennen *Eng* 59B7
Sens *France* 70C2
Seoul *S.Korea* 112G3
Seram I. *Indon.* 124E4
Sergino *Russia* 109H3
Sergipe State *Brazil* 37F4
Sérifos *Greece* 81E3
Serov *Russia* 109H4
Serpukhov *Russia* 102E4
Sérrai *Greece* 81E2
Sétif *Alg.* 141D4
Setúbal *Port.* 73A2
Sevastopol' *Ukraine* 108E5

Severnaya Zemlya *Russia* 104L2
Severodvinsk *Russia* 102E3
Sevilla *Spain* 73A2
Seychelles Is. *Indian* 150F1
Seydhisfodhur *Iceland* 92C1
Sézanne *France* 70C2
Sfax *Tunisia* 141E3
'S-Gravenhage *Neth.* 84A2
Shado Shima I. *Japan* 115N7
Shahjahanpur *India* 126G3
Shakhty *Russia* 108F5
Shandong Province *China* 112F3
Shanghai *China* 114G3
Shangrao *China* 114F4
Shantou *China* 114F4
Shanxi Province *China* 112F3
Shaoguan *China* 114F4
Shaoxing *China* 114G4
Shaoyang *China* 114F4
Shapinsay I. *Scot* 61F1
Shashi *China* 114F3
Sheffield *Eng* 55F4
Shenyang *China* 112G2
Shetland Is. *Scot* 61J7
Shijiazhuang *China* 112F3
Shillong *India* 127H3
Shimizu *Japan* 115N9
Shingü *Japan* 115L10
Shīrāz *Iran* 131D3
Shizuoka *Japan* 115N9
Shkodër *Alb.* 82D2
Shreveport *USA* 20D2
Shrewsbury *Eng* 58E5
Shuangyashan *China* 113H2
Sialkot *Pak.* 126F2
Siauliai *Lithuania* 95E5
Sibenik *Cro.* 77D2
Siberut I. *Indon.* 122B4
Sibiu *Rom.* 88E3
Sibolga *Indon.* 122B3
Sibu *Malay.* 123D3
Sichuan Province *China* 117E3
Sicila *Italy* 79C3
Sidi Bel Abbés *Alg.* 141C3
Siedlce *Pol.* 86E2
Siegen *FRG* 90B2
Siena *Italy* 77C2
Sifnos *Greece* 81E3
Sigüenza *Spain* 72B1
Siguiri *Guinea* 144B1
Sikasso *Mali* 144B1
Sikinos *Greece* 81F3
Simeulue I. *Indon.* 122B4
Singkawang *Indon.* 123C3
Sintra *Port.* 73A2
Sioux Falls *USA* 17D1
Siping *China* 112G2
Sipora I. *Indon.* 122B4
Siracusa *Italy* 79D3
Síros *Greece* 81E3
Sisak *Cro.* 77D1
Sittwe *Myanmar* 118B1
Sivas *Turk.* 130B2
Sjaelland I. *Den.* 94C4
Skara *Sweden* 94C4
Skegness *Eng* 55H4
Skellefteå *Sweden* 93E3
Skiáthos I. *Greece* 81E3
Skien *Nor.* 94B4

Skikda *Alg.* 141D3
Skiros *Greece* 81E3
Skópelos *Greece* 81E3
Skopje *Mac.* 82E2
Skovorodino *Russia* 106O4
Skye I. *Scot* 60B3
Sligo *Ireland* 64C2
Sliven *Bulg.* 83F2
Sobral *Brazil* 37E3
Société, Is. de la *French Pol.* 165
Socotra I. *Rep.Yemen* 133D4
Sodankylä *Fin* 93F2
Södertälje *Sweden* 94D4
Söderhamn *Sweden* 94D3
Sofia *Bulg.* 82E2
Sokodé *Togo* 145D2
Sokoto *Nig.* 145D1
Solápur *India* 128F4
Sollefteå *Sweden* 92D3
Solomon Is. *Pacific O.* 156F2
Somerset I. *Canada* 14J2
Sondrio *Italy* 76B1
Songkhla *Thai.* 122C3
Sorocaba *Brazil* 38F5
Sorong *Indon.* 124F4
Soroti *Uganda* 146G4
Sorrento *Italy* 79C2
Sorsele *Sweden* 92D2
Sosnowiec *Pol.* 88D2
Soudail *France* 69C3
Sŏul *S.Korea* 112G3
Sousse *Tunisia* 141E3
Southampton I. *Canada* 14K3
Southampton *Eng* 56F7
South Aust. State *Aus* 154C3
South Carolina State *USA* 18E2
South Dakota State *USA* 17C1
Southend-on-Sea *Eng* 56H6
South Georgia I.
  South Atlantic O. 39G8
South Island. *NZ* 157F5
Southport *Eng* 55G3
South Ronaldsay *Scot* 61F2
South Shields *Eng* 54F3
South Uist I. *Scot* 60A3
Sovetskaya Gavan'
  Russia 107Q5
Soweto *S.Africa* 149C3
Spalding *Eng* 55G5
Split *Cro.* 77D2
Spokane *USA* 16B1
Spratly Islands
  S.China Sea 119D2
Springfield *USA* 18D2
Springfield *USA* 18E2
Springs *S.Africa* 149C3
Srinagar *India* 126F2
S.Ronaldsay *Scot* 61F2
S.Severo *Italy* 77D2
Sta.Cruz de Tenerife
  Canary Is. 140B4
Stafford *Eng* 53E5
St.Albans *Eng* 56G6
St.Andrews *Scot* 63F4
Stanley *Falkland Is.* 39D8
Stara Zagora *Bulg.* 83F2
Starbuck I. *Kiribati* 162
St.Austell *Eng* 59C7

Stavanger Nor.	94B4	
Stavropol' Russia	108F5	
St.Brieuc France	68B2	
St.Croix I. Caribbean	26F3	
St.David's Wales	58B6	
St.Denis Réunion	151F4	
St.Dizier France	70C2	
Steinkjer Nor.	92C3	
Stewart I. NZ	157F5	
St.Gaudens France	69C3	
St.George's Grenada	27G4	
St.Helens Eng	53E4	
St.Helier Jersey	59E8	
Stirling Scot	62E4	
St.Ives Eng	59B7	
St.John Canada	15M5	
St.John's Antigua	26G3	
St.John's Canada	15N5	
St.Kitts Is. Caribbean	26G3	
St.Lawrence I. USA	22J	
St.Louis Sen.	140B5	
St.Louis USA	20E3	
St.Lucia I. Caribbean	27G4	
St.Malo France	68B2	
St.Martin Caribbean	26G3	
St.Mary's Eng	59A8	
St.Nazaire France	68B2	
St.Paul USA	18D1	
St.Peter Port Guernsey	59E8	
St.Petersburg Russia	102E4	
St.Petersburg USA	20E3	
St.Quentin France	70C2	
Stockport Eng	53E4	
Stoke-on-Trent Eng	53E4	
Stonehaven Scot	63F4	
Stören Nor.	92C3	
Storlien Sweden	92C3	
Stornoway Scot	60B2	
Storuman Sweden	92D2	
Strabane N.Ire.	65D2	
Stralsund FRG	85C2	
Stranraer Scot	62D6	
Strasbourg France	70D2	
Stratford-on-Avon Eng	56F5	
Streymoy I. Den.	92A2	
Strömsund Sweden	92D3	
Stronsay I. Scot	61F1	
Stroud Eng	56E6	
St.Tropez France	71D3	
Stuttgart FRG	90B3	
St.Vincent I. Caribbean	27G4	
Subotica Yugos.	82D1	
Suceava Rom.	89F3	
Sucre Bolivia	35C4	
Suduroy I. Den.	92A2	
Suez Egypt	142G2	
Sukhumi Georgia	108F5	
Sukkur Pak.	126E3	
Sulawesi Indon.	124E4	
Sulu Arch. Phil.	120E3	
Sumba I. Indon.	123D4	
Sumbawa I. Indon.	123D4	
Sumen Bulg.	83F2	
Sumy Ukraine	108E4	
Sunderland Eng	54F3	
Sundsvall Sweden	92D3	
Suntar Russia	106N3	
Surabaya Indon.	123D4	
Surakarta Indon.	123D4	
Surat India	128F3	
Surgut Russia	109J3	
Surtsey I. Iceland	92A2	
Suva Fiji	165	
Suzhou China	114G3	
Svalbard Is. Nor.	103C2	
Sveg Sweden	94C3	
Sverdrup Is. Canada	12H2	
Svetozarevo Yugos.	82E2	
Swakopmund S.Africa	149B3	
Swan I. Honduras	24C3	
Swansea Wales	58D6	
Swaziland, Kingdom		
Indep.S.Africa	151D3	
Swindon Eng	56F6	
Sydney Aust.	157E4	
Syktyvkar Russia	103G3	
Syracuse USA	18F1	
Syzran' Russia	108F4	
Szczecin Pol.	85C2	
Szczecinek Pol.	85D2	
Szeged Hung.	88E3	
Székesfehérvár Hung.	88D3	
Szekszárd Hung.	88D3	
Szolnok Hung.	88E3	

T

Tabora Tanz.	146G5	
Tabriz Iran	131C2	
Tabuaeran I. Kiribati	162	
Tabuk S.Arabia	130B3	
Taegu S.Korea	113G3	
Taejon S.Korea	112G3	
Tahiti I. Pacific O.	162	
T'ai-pei Taiwan	120E1	
Tái-nan Taiwan	120E1	
Taiwan,Republic China	120E1	
Taiyuan China	112F3	
Ta'izz Rep.Yemen	132C4	
Takada Japan	115N8	
Takaoka Japan	115M8	
Takasaki Japan	115N8	
Takoradi Ghana	144B2	
Talavera de la Reina Spain	72B2	
Talca Chile	40B6	
Talcahuano Chile	40B6	
Tallahassee USA	20E2	
Tallinn Estonia	102D4	
Tamale Ghana	144B2	
Tamanrasset Alg.	141D4	
Tambacounda Sen.	140B5	
Tampa USA	20E3	
Tampico Mexico	23D3	
Tamworth Aust.	157E4	
Tanga Tanz.	147G5	
Tanger Mor.	140C3	
Tangshan China	112F3	
Tanna I. Vanuatu	156F2	
Tanta Egypt	142G1	
Taolanaro Madag.	151E3	
Tarābulus Libya	141E3	
Tarakan Indon./Malay.	123D3	
Tarancón Spain	79B1	
Taranto Italy	79D2	
Tarbert Ireland	66B4	
Tarbert Scot	60B3	
Tarbert Scot	52B2	
Tarbes France	69C3	
Tarcoola Aust.	155C4	
Tarfaya Mor.	140B4	
Tarnów Pol.	88E2	
Tarragona Spain	74C1	
Tarrasa Spain	74C1	
Tartu Estonia	122B3	
Tashkent Uzbekistan	109H5	
Taunton Eng	58D6	
Tavira Port.	73A2	
Tavoy Myanmar	118B2	
Tawau Malay.	123D3	
Tawitawi Phil.	120E3	
Tbilisi Georgia	108F5	
Tecuci Rom.	89F3	
Tegucigalpa Honduras	25B4	
Tehrān Iran	131D2	
Tehuantepec Mexico	20D4	
Tel Aviv Israel	130B2	
Telford Eng	58E5	
Telukbetung Indon.	123C4	
Temuco Chile	40B6	
Tenerife Canary Is.	140B4	
Tennant Creek Aust.	154C2	
Tennessee State USA	18E2	
Teófilo Otõni Brazil	37E4	
Teresina Brazil	37E3	
Termez Uzbekistan	109H6	
Termoli Italy	77C2	
Terni Italy	77C2	
Teruel Spain	74B1	
Tessalit Mali	141D4	
Tete Mozam.	150D2	
Tétouan Mor.	140C3	
Teviothead Scot	63F5	
Texas State USA	23C2	
Thásos I. Greece	81E2	
Thetford Eng	56H5	
Thiès Sen.	140B5	
Thimphu Bhutan	127G3	
Thionville France	70D2	
Thíra I. Greece	81F3	
Thival Greece	81E3	
Thiviers France	69C2	
Thon Buri Thai.	118C2	
Thule Greenland	14M2	
Thunder Bay Canada	15K5	
Thurles Ireland	67D4	
Thurso Scot	61E2	
Thurston I. Ant.	170	
Tianjin China	112F3	
Tianshui China	117E3	
Tibet, Autonomous Region		
China	116C3	
Tidjikdja Maur.	140B5	
Tierp Sweden	94D3	
Tierra del Fuego I. Arg.	41C8	
Tierra del Fuego State Arg	41C8	
Tijuana USA	16B2	
Tilburg Neth.	84A2	
Tilos Greece	81F3	
Timbákion Greece	81E3	
Timimoun Alg.	141D4	
Timisoara Rom.	88E3	
Timor Indon.	124E4	
Tindouf Alg.	140C4	
Tipperary Ireland	66C4	
Tiranë Alb.	80D2	

Tiree I. *Scot* 62B4
Tîrgu Mures *Rom.* 89E3
Tiruchirāppalli *India* 128F4
Titov Veles *Macedonia* 82E2
Toamasina *Madag.* 150E2
Tobago I. *Caribbean Sea* 27G4
Tobermory *Scot* 62B4
Tobol'sk *Russia* 109H4
Tokelau Is. *Pacific O.* 165
Tokushima *Japan* 113H3
Tokyo *Japan* 115H9
Toledo *Spain* 72B2
Toledo *Italy* 18E1
Toliara *Madag.* 151E3
Tombouctou *Mali* 140C5
Tomsk *Russia* 109K4
Tonbridge *Eng* 56H6
Tonga Is. *Pacific O.* 165
Tonghua *China* 112G2
Tongling *China* 114F3
Tongue *Scot* 60D4
Toowoomba *Aust.* 156E3
Topeka *USA* 17D2
Tordesillas *Spain* 72A1
Torino *Italy* 76B1
Tornio *Fin* 93E2
Toronto *Canada* 15L5
Torquay *Eng* 59D7
Torreón *Mexico* 23C3
Torridon *Scot* 60C3
Tortosa *Spain* 74C1
Torun *Pol.* 86D2
Tóshavn *Faroes* 92A2
Tottori *Japan* 115L9
Touggourt *Alg.* 141D3
Toulon *France* 71D3
Toulouse *France* 69C3
Tourcoing *France* 70C1
Tours *France* 68C2
Tovalu Is. *Pacific O.* 165
Townsville *Aust.* 156D2
Toyama *Japan* 115M8
Toyohashi *Japan* 115M9
Tozeur *Tunisia* 141D3
Trabzon *Turk.* 130B1
Tralee *Ireland* 66B4
Trangan I. *Indon.* 124F4
Trapani *Italy* 78C3
Trenton *USA* 19F1
Trincomalee *Sri Lanka* 129G5
Trinidad *Caribbean Sea* 27G4
Tripoli *Libya* 141E3
Tripolis *Greece* 80E3
Tromsö *Nor.* 93D2
Trondheim *Nor.* 92C3
Trowbridge *Eng* 59E6
Troyes *France* 70C2
Trujillo *Peru* 35B3
Truro *Eng* 59B7
Tsetserleg *Mongolia* 111E2
Tsuchiura *Japan* 115P9
Tsumeb *Namibia* 149B2
Tsuruga *Japan* 115M9
Tsuruoka *Japan* 115N7
Tuamotu Is. *Pacific* 162
Tubruq *Libya* 142F1
Tubuai Is. *Pacific O.* 162
Tucson *USA* 23B2

Tucuman State *Arg.* 40C5
Tudela *Spain* 74B1
Tula *Russia* 102E4
Tullamore *Ireland* 67D3
Tulsa *USA* 17D2
Tunis *Tunisia* 141E3
Turda *Rom.* 88E3
Turks Is. *Caribbean Sea* 26E2
Turku *Fin* 95E3
Turnelf Is. *Belize* 24B3
Tuticorin *India* 128F5
Tuvalu Is. *Pacific O.* 165
Tuzla *Bos.Herz.* 82D2
Tver' *Russia* 102E4
Tyumen' *Russia* 109H4
Tyy *Spain* 72A1

U

Uberaba *Brazil* 37E4
Udaipur *India* 128F3
Uddevalla *Sweden* 94C4
Ufa *Russia* 109G4
Uig *Scot* 60B3
Ujung Pandang *Indon.* 123D4
Ukhta *Russia* 103G3
Ul'yanovsk *Russia* 108F4
Ulaanbaatar *Mongolia* 111E2
Ulan Ude *Russia* 106M4
Ullapool *Scot* 60C3
Ulm *FRG* 90B3
Umeå *Sweden* 93E3
Umtata *S.Africa* 149C4
Ungava Pen. *Canada* 15L3
Unimark I. *USA* 22J
Unst I. *Scot* 61K7
Upington *S.Africa* 149C3
Uppsala *Sweden* 94D4
Ural'sk *Kazakhstan* 108G4
Urgench *Uzbekistan* 108H5
Urosevac *Yugos.* 82E2
Ürümqi *China* 110C2
Urziceni *Rom.* 83F2
Üsküdar *Turk.* 130A1
Ussuriysk *Russia* 107P5
Ust' Kamchatsk *Russia* 105S4
Ust' Nera *Russia* 105Q3
Usti *Czech. Rep.* 91C2
Utah State *USA* 17B2
Utiel *Spain* 75B2
Utrecht *Neth.* 84A2
Utsjoki *Fin* 93F2
Utsunomiya *Japan* 115N8

V

Vaasa *Fin* 93E3
Vadodara *India* 128F3
Vaduz *Liech.* 70D2
Valdepeñas *Spain* 73B2
Valence *France* 71C3
Valencia *Spain* 75B2
Valencia *Ven.* 34C1
Valencia de Alcántara *Spain* 73A2
Valencia Region *Spain* 75B2
Valenciennes *France* 70C1
Valladolid *Spain* 72B1
Valledupar *Colombia* 34B1
Valletta *Malta* 141E3
Valls *Spain* 74C1
Valparaíso *Chile* 40B6

Vancouver *Canada* 13F5
Vancouver I. *Canada* 13F5
Vang *Nor.* 94B3
Vännäs *Sweden* 93D3
Vannes *France* 68B2
Vantaa *Fin* 95F3
Vanuatu Is. *Pacific O.* 156F2
Vārānasi *India* 127G3
Varazdin *Cro.* 77D1
Vardö *Nor.* 93G1
Varna *Bulg.* 83F2
Varnamo *Sweden* 94C4
Västerås *Sweden* 94D4
Västervik *Sweden* 94D4
Vasto *Italy* 77C2
Växjö *Sweden* 94C4
Veliko Turnovo *Bul* 83F2
Vellore *India* 129F4
Veracruz *Mexico* 23D4
Vereeniging *S.Africa* 149C3
Verín *Spain* 72A1
Vermont State *USA* 19F1
Versailles *France* 68C2
Vestmannaeyjar I. *Iceland* 92A2
Viana do Castelo *Port.* 72A1
Vibo Valentia *Italy* 79D3
Victoria *China* 119D1
Victoria I. *Canada* 12G2
Victoria State *Aust.* 157D4
Videle *Rom.* 83F2
Vidin *Bulg.* 82E2
Viella *Spain* 74C1
Vienna *Aust.* 91D3
Vientiane *Laos* 118C2
Vierzon *France* 68C2
Vigo *Spain* 72A1
Vijayawada *India* 129G4
Vila *Vanuatu.* 156F2
Vila Nova de Gaia *Por.* 72A1
Vila Real *Port.* 72A1
Villach *Aust.* 91C3
Vilnius *Lithuania* 102D4
Viña del Mar *Chile* 40B6
Vinh *Viet.* 119C2
Vinnitsa *Ukraine* 102D5
Virgin Is. *Caribbean* 26G3
Virginia State *USA* 18F2
Vis I. *Cro.* 77D2
Visby *Sweden* 95D4
Vishakhapatnam *India* 129G4
Viterbo *Italy* 77C2
Vitória *Brazil* 38F5
Vitoria *Spain* 72B1
Vitry-le-François *Fra* 70C2
Vladimir *Russia* 102F4
Vladivostok *Russia* 107P5
Vlorë *Alb.* 80D2
Volgograd *Russia* 108F5
Vologda *Russia* 102F4
Vólos *Greece* 80E3
Vorkuta *Russia* 103H3
Voronezh *Russia* 108E5
Voroshilovgrad *Ukraine* 108E5
Voss *Nor.* 94B3
Vranje *Yugos.* 82E2
Vratsa *Bulg.* 82E2
Vrbovsko *Cro.* 77D1
Vrsac *Yugos.* 82E1

W

Wadi Halfa *Sudan*	142G2
Wad Medani *Sudan*	146G3
Wagga Wagga *Aust.*	157D4
Wahiawa *Hawaiian Is.*	22H
Waigeo I. *Indon.*	124F4
Wailuka *Hawaiian Is.*	22H
Wakayama *Japan*	115L9
Wake I. *Pacific O.*	159
Wakkanai *Japan*	113J2
Wallis and Futuna Is. *Pacific O.*	165
Walsall *Eng*	56F5
Walvis Bay *Namibia*	149B3
Wanganui *NZ*	157G4
Warangal *India*	128F4
Warley *Eng*	56F5
Warminster *Eng*	59E6
Warrnambool *Aust.*	155D4
Warsaw *Pol.*	86E2
Warwick *Eng*	56F5
Washington DC *USA*	19F2
Washington State *USA*	16A1
Waterford *Ireland*	67D4
Watford *Eng*	56G6
Wau *PNG*	125G4
Wau *Sudan*	146F4
Weifang *China*	112F3
Welkom *S.Africa*	149C3
Wellesley Is. *Aust.*	154C2
Wellington *NZ*	157G5
Welshpool *Wales*	58D5
Wenzhou *China*	114G4
Wesel *FRG*	84B2
Wessel Is. *Aust.*	154C2
West Bromwich *Eng*	56F5
Western Aust. State *Aust.*	154B3
Western Isles *Scot*	60A3
Western Samoa *Pacific O.*	165
West Falkland I. *South Atlantic*	41C8
West Indies, Is. *Caribbean Sea*	26F2
Weston-super-Mare *Eng*	58E6
Westport *Ireland*	64B3
Westray I. *Scot*	61E1
West Virginia State *USA*	18E2
Wetar I. *Indon.*	124E4
Wewak *PNG*	125G4
Wexford *Ireland*	67E4
Weymouth *Eng*	59E7
Whalsay I. *Scot*	61K7
Whangarei *NZ*	157G4
Whitby *Eng*	55G3
Whitchurch *Eng*	53E5
Whitehaven *Eng*	53D3
Whitehorse *Canada*	12E3
Whyalla *Aust.*	155C4
Wichita *USA*	17D2
Wick *Scot*	61E2
Wicklow *Ireland*	67E4
Widnes *Eng*	53E4
Wigan *Eng*	53E4
Wilhelmshaven *FRG*	84B2
Wilmington *USA*	19F2
Wilmslow *Eng*	53E4
Winchester *Eng*	56F6
Windhoek *Namibia*	149B3
Windsor *Eng*	56G6
Winnemucca *USA*	16A1
Winnipeg *Canada*	13J5
Wisconsin State *USA*	18D1
Wloclawek *Pol.*	86D2
Wokam I. *Indon.*	124F4
Wolfsburg *FRG*	85C2
Wollongong *Aust.*	157E4
Wolverhampton *Eng*	58E5
Wŏnsan *N.Korea*	112G3
Worcester *Eng*	58E5
Worcester *S.Africa*	149B4
Workington *Eng*	52D3
Worksop *Eng*	55F4
Worthing *Eng*	57G7
Wrexham *Wales*	53E4
Wroclaw *Pol.*	91D2
Wuhan *China*	114F3
Wuhu *China*	114F3
Würzburg *FRG*	90B3
Wuxi *China*	114G3
Wuzhou *China*	114F4
Wyndham *Aust.*	154B2
Wyoming State *USA*	17C1

X

Xai Xai *Mozam.*	151D3
Xi'an *China*	117E3
Xiamen *China*	114F4
Xiangfan *China*	114F3
Xiangtan *China*	114F4
Xingtai *China*	112F3
Xining *China*	111E3
Xinjiang Uygur Zizhiqu Prov. *China*	110C2
Xinxiang *China*	114F3
Xinyang *China*	114F3
Xuchang *China*	114F3
Xuzhou *China*	114F3

Y

Ya'an *China*	117E3
Yakutsk *Russia*	104O3
Yamagata *Japan*	115P7
Yamdena I. *Indon.*	124F4
Yamoussoukro *Cote d'Ivoire*	144B2
Yangon *Myanmar*	118B2
Yangquan *China*	112F3
Yangzhou *China*	114F3
Yantai *China*	112G3
Yaoundé *Cameroon*	145E4
Yap I. *Pacific O.*	121F3
Yapen I. *Indon.*	125F4
Yaroslavl' *Russia*	102E4
Yazd *Iran*	131D2
Ye *Myanmar*	118B2
Yekaterinburg *Russia*	109H4

Yell I. *Scot*	61J7
Yellowknife *Canada*	12G3
Yeniseysk *Russia*	106L4
Yeovil *Eng*	58E7
Yerevan *Armenia*	108F5
Yibin *China*	117E4
Yichang *China*	114F3
Yinchuan *China*	111E3
Yingkou *China*	112G2
Yiyang *China*	114F4
Yogyakarta *Indon.*	123D4
Yokkaichu *Japan*	115M9
Yokohama *Japan*	115N9
Yokosuka *Japan*	115N9
York *Eng*	55F4
Youghal *Ireland*	67D4
Ystad *Sweden*	94C4
Yukon Territory State *Can*	12E3
Yumen *China*	111D2
Yunnan Province *China*	117E4
Yuzhno-Sakhalinsk *Russia*	107Q5

Z

Zaandam *Neth.*	84A2
Zadar *Cro.*	77D2
Zafra *Spain*	73A2
Zagreb *Cro.*	77D1
Zähedän *Iran*	131E3
Zákinthos I. *Greece*	80E3
Zamboanga *Phil.*	120E3
Zamora *Spain*	72A1
Zanzibar I. *Tanz.*	147G5
Zaporozh'ye *Ukraine*	108E5
Zaragón Region *Spain*	74B1
Zaragoza *Spain*	74B1
Zaysan *Kazakhstan*	109K5
Zemlya Frantsa Iosifa Is. *Barents Sea*	103G1
Zenica *Bos. Herz.*	82D2
Zhangjiakou *China*	112F2
Zhangzhou *China*	114F4
Zhanjiang *China*	114F4
Zhdavov *Ukraine*	108E5
Zhejiang Province *China*	114F4
Zhengzhou *China*	114F3
Zhenjiang *China*	114F3
Zhitomir *Ukraine*	102D4
Zhuzhou *China*	114F4
Zibo *China*	112F3
Zielona Gora *Pol.*	85D2
Ziguinchor *Sen.*	140B5
Zilina *Slovakia*	88D3
Zinder *Niger*	145D1
Zlatoust *Russia*	109G4
Znojmo *Czech. Rep.*	91D3
Zomba *Malawi*	150D2
Zouerate *Maur.*	140B4
Zunyi *China*	117E4
Zurich *Switz.*	70D2
Zwickau *FRG*	91C2

Published 2007 by Geddes & Grosset,
David Dale House, New Lanark ML11 9DJ, Scotland

© 2002 Geddes & Grosset

First published 2002
Reprinted 2003, 2005, 2007

ISBN 978 1 85534 270 9

Printed and bound in India